ROOTS
& RIVERS

Timeless Principles of Life and
Business from the Power of PLACE

KIM STROHMEIER

Kim Strohmeier's *Roots & Rivers* is a beautiful tapestry of real-life stories from which he has brilliantly abstracted five timeless principles of life and business. From his years of observing, trying, failing and adjusting, he has learned how to triumph and to coach others to do the same. I've known and respected Kim for more than 40 years. This is a great book! Get your copy and utilize these golden nuggets to make your business all that it can be.

– Dallas R. Stafford, Businessman and Retired Banker

In *Roots & Rivers*, business coach and strategist Kim Strohmeier uses the moving power of story to teach and encourage business owners to make the changes that promote greater success, satisfaction, and meaning. With wisdom and tenderness, he accompanies the reader through some of the mistakes, hard conversations, and risks a business owner may face. As both a millennial and a recent first-time business owner, I am grateful for the wisdom Kim has to offer.

– Jeff Mazzone, MA, LPC, MA - Licensed Professional Counselor & Co-Founder/Co-Owner of *Harmonia Counseling Group*

It is an honor for me to recommend Kim's book, *Roots & Rivers*. I have known Kim from the early years of his very successful career. I count his Dad and Mom among my dearest friends. I know his PLACE. I have been on Elkhorn Creek in one of his canoes. You will find his book not only refreshing, but extremely insightful. This is not a digest written from research in a library. It is valuable time-tested principles acquired in the School of his own multifaceted experience. You will find it to be a down-to-earth Pathway to Success! Read and be blessed!

– Lucian Robinson, Pastor, *Garner Church of Christ*

Kim Strohmeier's new book *Roots & Rivers* shares inspirational stories that provide profound truths for building successful businesses. He builds upon his successful career of coaching and instructing business teams across all types of products and industries. He applies his strengths of taking ideas and theory and building simple, usable how-to paths that business owners can immediately put to work. For me, Kim provides the much needed HOW of Forbes' former executive editor Rich Karlgaard's book *Life 2.0: how people across America are transforming their lives by finding the where of their happiness.*

– Sharon Ballard, science and technology multiple start-up CEO, instructor, coach, and author of *Supercoach® Entrepreneurial Training*, and *Introduction to the SBIR/STTR Program: A Brief Introduction to the Small Business Innovation Research (SBIR) and Small Business Technology Transfer (STTR) Program*

Kim Strohmier's book "*Roots & Rivers*" is a must-read for any business owner. The ability to plan and adapt to the changing currents is what helps people survive life on the river, the same skills that allow businesses to survive the varying currents of the market. Kim weaves his life at his homeplace with vivid scenes that tie together business planning and life lessons. Just as rivers wind through the countryside and change with the seasons, so do our businesses face good times and storms. Sage advice and excellent storytelling.

– Lou Kelley, MA, PMP, Founder, Owner, and Coach, *The Honing Stone*

I've known Kim Strohmeier since the 1980's when he became (what we referred to as) the county agent in Owen County, KY. His excellent observation and listening skills were evident from the start.

By developing a deep understanding of practices and problems, Kim was able to make connections between farmers and recognized experts to find answers to many agricultural and business problems we faced. Throughout his years as our county agent, Kim developed a wealth of knowledge, experience, and strong relationships. He was well-respected and known as the go-to person for having the answers and giving sound advice on the spot. Now, with this new book, *Roots & Rivers*, he is continuing to share many valuable insights well worth learning.

– Steven Malcomb, retired site supervisor, *Dow Corning*

As a long-time business owner, I tend to be cynical about business books and the non-relevant and non-achievable advice often given. *Roots & Rivers* weaves real-life events of the author into actual small business challenges that any business owner would recognize. I thoroughly enjoyed it, and I learned quite a bit, as well. The author does a wonderful job telling an interesting story and offering a comprehensive business framework, including planning tools that are completely relatable and effective in creating and growing any small family business. I believe a small business is a living organism, and needs to be approached as such. Kim's book treats it that way. And it's a fun read too!

– Ann Wingrove, 35-year owner, *Completely Kentucky Inc.*

I am so excited to endorse *Roots & Rivers* by Kim Strohmeier. He has a way of not only looking at the business side of a situation, but the personal side as well. You will see this time and time again throughout the book, including the chapter on "Remodeling the Homestead". Kim brings home the point that sometimes in business, and in life, you can't do it all yourself, and that's ok. I hope when you read Kim's book you will gain as much insight into your business and personal life as I did. Kim has been our company business coach several times throughout the years. I am proud that he has taken the time to put down his knowledge and compassion into *Roots & Rivers*.

– **Suzanne Ellerbrock, Owner, President, and Certified Senior Move Manager,** *Golden Bridges*

Most business books tell you how to grow faster. This one teaches you how to grow right. *Roots & Rivers* connects business, family, and purpose in a way that feels real because it is. The stories about Uncle Eddie, a Marine Raider corpsman and hero, ground the book in something deeper than business and remind you what service, sacrifice, and legacy actually look like in a life well-lived. Kim Strohmeier uses honest experiences to show how planning, discipline, and reflection shape both your company and your character. It's not just about building a better business, it's about building a life you actually want to live while you run that business.

– **Michael P. Murphy, Force Recon Marine**

I had the opportunity to work with Kim for nine years, and I saw firsthand how he gained the utmost respect from our local farmers and community members who were always seeking his advice and leadership. During this time, his family started the remodel phase of the homeplace. I never understood why they wanted to be so close to the river with the fear of flooding until I saw the finished product. The many stories that I heard when visiting while we were looking over the river, I understood why he wanted to be at the homeplace. I know I drove him crazy whenever it rained a lot to let him know I would be there to help the moving process, in case of flooding. Now I understand that a family farm doesn't raise you - it reveals who you truly are. Through life's lessons we learn how to work, how to rest, how to live and how to be a great leader.

– **Stephanie Howard, Staff Assistant,** *Owen County Cooperative Extension Service*

Lately, I've found myself thinking more about purpose in my own business, as we've gotten through the initial growth stage. My colleague Kim Strohmeier's book, *Roots & Rivers,* sharpened how I think about progress, with less emphasis on speed or an eventual exit and more attention to what actually lasts. The idea of place as a stabilizing force, something that absorbs shock when conditions change, reframed how I see success over time. For me, it became a more honest measure of what we are building for ourselves and the people we serve.

– **Shannon Turner, co-owner,** *Meza Design*

Table of Contents

———

Principle Four: Cultivate Contentment

Principle Five: Execute with Excellence

Also by Kim Strohmeier

The Indispensable Start

Turn Your Business Into a Powerhouse

The House on Fifth Street

To all those who are responsible for my love of my Place. Thank you for your inspiration.

My parents:

Dave Strohmeier (1931–2025) and
Beth Strohmeier (1936–2019)

My uncle:

Edward Strohmeier Jr. (1924–2004)

My paternal grandparents:

Edward Strohmeier Sr. (1897–1969) and
Esther Strohmeier (1898–1981)

My maternal grandparents:

Lewis Crews (1907–1977) and
Hazel Crews (1909–1998)

". . . And in this place I will give you peace."

—Haggai 2:9 (NABRE)

The Importance of Place

Listen to stories of people who moved from the mountains of Appalachia decades ago to find work, and they still think of the mountains as their home. It's their Place.

In numerous small towns across the country, people identify with their home community. They graduate from high school, they get a job, they get married and raise a family, they go watch their kids play football on the same field they played on a generation ago. It's their Place.

People who have grown up along a stream and have been flooded out, they still go back. They laugh and say that they have river water running through their veins. It's their Place.

My father-in-law was born in a house his grandparents built for his parents, right across the street from the Catholic church where he was baptized and confirmed, where he got married, where his grandkids were baptized, and where his family attended his funeral. With the exception of a couple years' worth of seeing the South Pacific, compliments of the US Army, he lived in that house his entire life and was buried in the cemetery right across from his front door. It was his Place.

My long-time friend Rob Worden moved around a lot as he was growing up. His dad was a manufacturing lobbyist his whole career, and they would stay no more than five or six years in one town. We didn't see much of each other, yet we remained close. But he didn't have a place he could call his own.

Shortly after I graduated from college, he told me, "Kim, I envy you and your life. You've got roots. I've moved around all over the country, but I don't really feel I can call any place home. You do. You've got a home base."

Recently, I called and asked him if he remembered that conversation. He did, and he added, "Roots act like a cushion, a means of support you can't see. It seems to me that when you have a place, the wind doesn't blow quite as hard, and the winters aren't quite as cold."

Through those conversations, I realized just how important Place is to our lives.

That's what this book is about. Place.

The Backdrop for the Story

In 1938, my grandfather bought a farm and fishing camp on a river near the capital city of Frankfort, Kentucky. My dad was six years old when they moved, and he lived there for eighty-seven years, the rest of his life—a feat of longevity that is seldom replicated. It was his homeplace.

I grew up there with my brother. The farm, the river, the creek, and my grandparents' home were part of our lives. We irrigated crops from the creek. We jumped in the water to cool off after working in hay on a hot summer day. We took a rowboat across the river to a big sandbar to go swimming. We went fishing with both our granddads. We explored the hill behind our house, and as all self-respecting Kentucky boys do, we shot basketball with our friends at the goal in front of our house.

I lived away from my homeplace for twenty-five years as an adult, but I visited home often. After my family and I moved back to my homeplace in 2007, I realized: Though I'd owned a house in another community for twenty years, that house was never really home. This was. This was my Place.

And my Place has taught me many lessons about life and about business.

The Power of a Story

Over the years, I've learned that stories carry a lot of weight. My father-in-law told stories about his time as a post office clerk in Guadalcanal during World War II, and he held us spellbound for hours. My ten-year-old son was so impressed with one of these stories about a week of KP duty that he used it as the subject of a 4-H speech fifty years after it happened. My Uncle Eddie, whom you will meet later in this book, had his own World War II stories about the Battle of Okinawa, and I still shudder at the tales of the three months of absolute hell he lived through.

In my role as a business coach over the last twenty years, I've worked with people in all kinds of businesses, and I've noticed that no matter how much training someone has, stories and experiences are what really stick with them. A mistake that cost a whole lot more than money, or a hard conversation they avoided until it was too late, or a risk they finally took that paid off. What really shaped them came in the form of stories.

This is true for me as well.

This book is a collection of some of those moments from my life. They helped me grow, and shaped how I see life and work.

You might be carrying a full load now – trying to run a business, take care of people who depend on you, and still find some time for yourself. I believe that some of my experiences might help you to see your own situation differently. Or maybe it'll help you feel a little less alone in your own challenges.

These stories come from my homeplace. Not just the land and the streams but the people, the seasonal rhythms of work and play, and the quiet lessons that come from paying attention (and, oftentimes, not paying attention when I should have).

These stories relate to my roots, to my Place. They've taught me about things worth holding onto—about people, about life and family, about character and faith, about dealing with challenges, about how business really works, and about how to keep going when things don't work out as you've planned. Some are funny when I look back on them, though they weren't so much at the time. Some still bring a lump to my throat. Some of them taught me lessons I didn't know I needed.

The Power of Place

I've noticed that Place seems to be important to people who, like my friend Rob, do not particularly have ties to a certain geographic location. I've recently moved away from my homeplace to another state. Where I live now, a lot of my current friends and neighbors come from very transient military families, and when I meet someone who moved a lot growing up, I'll sense a bit of wistfulness in their voice when they say they're not really from anywhere.

Place transcends geography. It's the kitchens where everyone gathered, where everyday life was lived, where stories were told. In my case, it's the farm where I learned how to work. It's the back roads I traveled hundreds of times taking my kids to ball or cheerleading practice, listening to music together with them and sharing conversations along the way. It's the hillside behind my house that I walked through when I needed to clear my head. It's the driveway where my dad taught me how to change the oil or fix a tire. It's the church where I found my faith, and the rock bar in the creek where I got baptized.

Place holds memories. I have photos of my grandmother lovingly tending to her flowers in a way I tried to emulate forty years later. I recall the tree, long gone, that I used to climb up into with a book tucked under my arm. My Place gives me a sense of connection, and I notice that my kids, even now, hold a close connection to our homeplace.

I've had some successes and a lot of failures—in actions, in results, and in character. All these lessons have worked together to make me who I am. The way I work, these lessons I learned, the things I do to relax—all of them started at my Place.

Intersection of Story and Place

My physical place is a 160-acre farm in northern Franklin County, Kentucky, that is bordered by the Kentucky River, right where the Elkhorn Creek flows into the river. The Elkhorn serves as the watershed for nearly the entire central Bluegrass region of the state, including the small city of Lexington, Kentucky. The farm is largely enclosed by a big horseshoe bend in the creek, just before it flows into the river. The workplace was a fishing camp that my grandparents ran, as well as a tobacco and cattle farm that my dad owned in my earlier years, one that he turned into a campground and marina when he was about fifty years old.

My place was also a playground. We lived within hollering distance of my grandparents' house, which is always a good thing. When chores or farmwork were done, my brother Kevin and I would ride our bikes and go visit the weekend fishing camp visitors. We'd get in one of my granddad's rowboats and go over to the sandbar on the opposite side of the river. We'd water ski, and go hiking, exploring, swimming, and canoeing.

As an adult, I didn't live very far away, so I'd go back often, either to help Dad or to visit and continue some of the same play I did as a kid. I realized then that this wasn't just a workplace or a place to play. It was my Place. It's part of my identity. It's made me who I am and shaped how I see the world. It's taught me lessons that have shaped how I run my coaching business today and how I work with business owners.

Without my Place and my people, I wouldn't have these stories. I wouldn't have these experiences to share with you as a guide for navigating life and business.

Place as a Metaphor for Business

Running a business is a lot like tending to a place you care about. When Place is important, you look after it; you care for it. You notice when something's not quite right, and you tend to what's been previously neglected. It's the same with a business. It requires attention. Not just to the immediate fires that need putting out, but to the things that quietly change over time, the things that look fine now but will cause trouble if ignored.

This care of your Place takes a lot of effort and a lot of work. Because of that, your life and your time are intimately tied to the details of both your Place and your business. Even when the work slows down and you have time to breathe, once you sit down on the porch to relax, you notice a weed growing in the flowerbed, and you have to get up and get rid of it. Then you find another weed, and then you notice a stray overgrown branch, and before you know it, you've got the pruners in hand to fix it. You just can't help it.

It's the same with your business. Even when you're sitting outside on a Saturday afternoon with a glass of sweet tea or a bourbon, supposedly relaxing, you're still thinking about your business, mulling over a problem or an opportunity. You just can't help it.

Place teaches limits. A physical place has boundaries of some kind. It might be invisible, like the boundary between you and your neighbor's yard. It might be fences, roads, or, such as in my case, a stream. Something that indicates you only have so much space. More than that, you only have so much time and energy to devote to your space.

A well-tended place gets handed down; it outlasts the one who served it as caretaker. Before I was a business coach, I had a long-time role as a farm advisor, and I knew a lot of farmers who believed that they had a responsibility to leave their farm in better shape than when they got it. And we all know leaders who are singularly driven to improve the community where they live and work.

The best business owners have the same mindset: They build a business that is solid, something that's worth passing on.

Place reminds you that your work is part of something bigger.

PLACE as a Framework

While every business has its own unique features and personality, there is a basic framework that each one uses. It starts with the business owner's idea and the planning that goes into making it viable. Then there are the products, services, and efforts that go into generating income for that business, followed by the challenge of developing a team of people that can help make the business successful. It also involves the actual operations of the business: the actions the business owner takes to make all the above efforts work.

Through all this, the business owner recognizes that he or she has a life outside the business, and that the business is there not only to provide a needed service to others, but to provide a good life for themselves.

From my years of observing, trying, failing, and adjusting, I've developed a framework I use with clients to help them build steady, thoughtful growth. That framework spells out PLACE, with each letter representing a key area on which every business needs to focus:

P - Prepare the Plan - The efforts you take in building the design for the business.

L - Leverage Your Livelihood - The ways in which the money comes into the business.

A - Assemble and Align Your Team - How you train and guide the people that will support you.

C - Cultivate Contentment - Your efforts in making time for self, satisfaction, and purpose.

E - Execute with Excellence - The work it takes to keep everything moving smoothly.

Each chapter in this book will connect to one of these five areas. I'll set the scene with a story, musing on what I've learned about business and life from that story, how others I've worked with have applied these lessons, and how you might consider doing the same. At the end of each chapter, you'll find a reflection question and additional tips to help you address it.

How You Might Benefit from PLACE

Let's do a bit of daydreaming.

Imagine what it would look like if your business worked perfectly.

You didn't start this thing on a whim. You had a dream, you had a skill, and you had a clear picture of meaningful work that would provide a service to your fellow man. You believed that not only would this business provide you with a gratifying way to make a living, it would ultimately provide you with freedom: economic freedom, because customers would eagerly buy what you offered, but also freedom of time, because you had a team of people who believed in what you do and were excited to come to work. Their efforts allowed you to get away to enjoy the fruits of your labor. You had a sense of peace and contentment because you had a business that worked.

But when you daydream, you eventually have to wake up and come back to reality. That reality may be that your this business hasn't worked out quite like you had planned, and that freedom seems out of reach. Daily fires need to be put out, paying the bills can be a constant struggle, and the steady pressure of it all keeps wearing you down.

Your thoughts may begin to sound like:

- "I'm just spinning my wheels, I'm barely able to make ends meet . . ."
- "I can't find good people that I can trust. If I'm gone for a day, the place falls apart . . ."
- "I feel like I'm in a rut. I'm not sure what I need to do to move forward . . ."
- "I've got too much to do and not enough time to do it . . ."
- "I haven't had the time to get out on the river for a year or more . . ."

I've voiced each of these frustrations. I know how draining it can be to feel stuck, to feel like you're stretched too thin and don't know what to do next. You need to feel in control again.

Think about what success might look like for you if your business worked the way you intended. This might sound like:

- Sales are good, and profits are consistent. You can sleep at night knowing you can easily make payroll, and you wake up with peace, knowing the bills are being paid and your business is working.
- You can leave the shop without worrying that everything's going to fall apart while you're gone. You've got a team of people that believe in what you're doing, and you trust them completely to take care of any problems before you ever hear of them.

- The possibilities for your business feel exciting, and you have a clear, workable plan that shows you exactly how to move forward and grow.

- Time belongs to you again. No more being chained to the store! You can take a long weekend without feeling guilty. You're enjoying the life you hoped for when you first started this business.

- You can take that bucket-list fishing trip to Voyageurs National Park. Your team is excited for you, and on their own they've adjusted their schedules to cover for you. You can easily afford it because sales have been great the last year, and you have perfect confidence that your business is in good hands while you're gone.

This is the business you were meant to build.

The stories in this book can show you how you can build the business that you first imagined and the life that you deserve. There's a way to plan ahead. There are decisions you can make now that can ease the burden later, helping you shift your focus to building something solid and sustainable, rather than getting lost in the day-to-day grind.

Building a meaningful business, and a meaningful life, doesn't happen by accident. It takes intention. It takes some trial and error. It takes a willingness to learn from your missteps and keep going.

If you're ready to get started, not just someday, but now, I'd like to help you take that first step. Before you even turn to the next page, you can schedule a time to talk with me. We'll look at where you are, where you want to go, and what stands in the way. There's no pressure, just a conversation to see what's possible.

If that sounds like something you need right now, visit www.25withKim.com or use the QR code below and book a call. I'll be happy to listen and help you work through it.

If you'd prefer to keep reading, I hope this book helps you see your own life and your own business more clearly, guiding you through whatever comes next.

Thanks for being here. Let's get started.

PRINCIPLE ONE
Prepare the Plan

*The Efforts You Take in Building
the Design for the Business*

For many years, being on a stream in a canoe or kayak has been a source of personal enjoyment and relaxation. But I've found that if I'm not in the proper type of craft, the sport can be a source of tremendous frustration.

Some canoes and kayaks are designed for whitewater. The structure of the boat allows the paddler to quickly move around rocks and other obstructions in the stream. Others are designed for lakes or other flat water. These boats have a keel, a structural member on the bottom of the hull from front to back, that allows it to move in a relatively straight line. Without it, all your paddling leaves you worn out and going in circles.

Running a business is a lot like that. Without planning, you might be working just as hard as you possibly can, but you never seem to get ahead. You're putting in the effort, but you aren't making much progress. A business plan is the keel that helps you move forward with purpose. Just as the right boat makes the difference between frustration and joy on the water, the right planning makes the difference between chaos and progress in your business.

For many people, the words "business plan" conjure up an image of a hundred-page document filled with jargon that sits on the shelf drawing dust. To avoid this perception, I call it a Start-Up Blueprint, because that's what it is: a blueprint of how you will start this business. It's a tool that steadies you and keeps you on course, laying out where you're trying to go and what you need to do to get there. It also helps you to be proactive, to shape your circumstances so you're not constantly reacting to them.

In this section, I'll describe various planning tools that will help you understand yourself and your business in an honest way. Taking a close look at your strengths and weaknesses can give you a clearer picture of where you can excel and where you might struggle. Identifying opportunities and threats can help you see how outside forces will affect your journey. We call this a SWOT analysis: it maps out the waters ahead, showing you where the rocks are, where the currents can carry you, and where you need to steer more carefully.

Another important part of planning is the systems you put in place. Work flows best when processes are set up to guide each step. A system for handling leads, a process for following up with customers, or a method for tracking inventory reduces mistakes and keeps the operation moving efficiently. Systems take the guesswork out of daily work and make it easier to see where things are off-track.

Planning also challenges the assumptions you may be carrying. These assumptions may turn into tendencies that sound like: *What I sell is good, and the customer likes it, and I don't need to make any changes*; or *I'm pretty well set in what I do, so costs aren't going to change much*; or *I've figured out how to deal with my competition, so I don't need to pay much attention to them anymore*. But assumptions, left untested, can cause you to drift badly off course. Addressing them helps you make decisions based on what is actually happening, not just what you hope is true.

Finally, good planning keeps you adaptable. The waters are always changing. Trends shift, customer expectations grow, and new opportunities open up. If you're not paying attention, you'll miss them. But if you build adaptability into your planning, you can adjust your course without losing momentum. You can be prepared and take advantage of what comes your way without panicking at every change.

In the chapters that follow, we'll walk through the tools that make up strong planning. You'll see how a business plan, a SWOT analysis, systemizing, tested assumptions, and awareness of trends all fit together to guide your work. With these in place, you can paddle with purpose, stay on course, and enjoy the journey of building a business that supports the life you want to live.

CHAPTER 1

Starting a Canoe Livery

Being on the river, I gravitated toward water sports growing up. I learned how to water ski in high school and loved that. I'd take my grandfather's rowboats to a nice sandbar on the other side of the river to go swimming. And I'd spend many a day on the Elkhorn Creek that borders a good portion of my dad's farm, wading in the creek and sitting on the massive rocks that had fallen from cliffs eons ago, listening to the water flowing over the riffles.

At some point, and I don't recall how, my brother and I conjured up an old canoe. Most likely, it floated downstream. It was in rough shape, and the previous owner probably didn't miss it much, but it opened a whole world of possibilities for me. I was now a real explorer!

In college, I took that title seriously. Some canoe liveries had started operations on a couple streams near me, and I started driving to them and exploring their waters. One such livery was on the Licking River, in Falmouth, Kentucky, (which flows into the Ohio River, right across from downtown Cincinnati.) I visited them several times, got to know the owners, and saw enough of the stream there to appreciate it, but I also believed my Place was prettier!

Going there whetted my entrepreneurial spirit. If they could do this, maybe I could too.

Shortly after my wife, Francie, and I married, we started a new canoe livery, the first one on the Elkhorn. We named it Still Waters Canoe Trails, after my dad's fledgling marina that he had started just upstream from the mouth of the creek. Francie designed a logo, and we bought ten aluminum canoes from a supplier. I had a local welder build me a ten-canoe carrier trailer that we could haul behind my dad's truck, and we built some seats for the back of the truck so we could carry both people and canoes upstream.

We managed to get some free publicity, including some local news media highlights, and all in all, we were pretty pleased with that first year. We were successful enough in that we purchased some more canoes. But by the end of that first year, some cracks started developing in our system.

Since this was essentially a weekend business, we were staying at my parents' house every weekend. Francie and I attended Mass at her home church Sunday mornings (about an hour away) so we didn't get back to my parents until early afternoon. While we were away, my dad had to take care of our canoe customers, so I started staying home, not attending church with Francie. This became a strain on our marriage, and while church wasn't all that important to me at the time, it was frustrating to Francie to have to go by herself.

As the business grew, we started getting more weekday rentals. Since I had a full-time job during the week, my dad had to completely take care of those customers. When our daughter was born in the winter of that first year, a newborn threw another challenge into the following season's business. I had to do more of it on my own, and Francie and I were apart many weekends.

After a couple more years of business growth, I realized I couldn't do both jobs. My part-time canoe livery was taking time away from my career and my family, and while I felt it had potential, the stress wasn't worth it, so we sold the livery to my dad.

It worked well for him. He continued to grow it, and it added an important element to his marina and campground. It gave him a competitive advantage over two other campgrounds nearby, and it gave us our first taste of running a business, satisfying my desire of doing something on the waters that I loved.

⬙

I had raised a tobacco crop as a tenant farmer for several years, but this canoe livery was the first time that I actually started a business. It was moderately successful, but looking back on it, we weren't equipped to run the business the way it should have been run, and I learned numerous lessons from it.

According to Michael Gerber, in his great book *The E-Myth Revisited*, we had what he called an entrepreneurial seizure. We started with a great idea, but we never thought through the ramifications of it. We knew what we were going to sell, and we were excited about that—we enjoyed canoeing ourselves, and we just knew other people would enjoy having the opportunity to get out on the water, but we didn't have a clue about determining our target market (which I'll talk about later).

We had a great core competency, which I'll also get into later. Compared to others, we had access to two streams, so we didn't have to go get people when they completed their trip. Being at the mouth of the stream, they came to us, but we weren't able to make full use of that advantage because of our other problems.

There were the family ramifications; my wife had a traditional nine-to-five workday during the week and got tired of working every weekend, and I didn't think through the endgame with my dad. I was using his land, his truck, his launch ramp, and during the week, his time, to operate my business. He didn't even charge me a percentage of the revenues for all those resources he provided.

All in all, we didn't know what a business plan was. And that was unfortunate. We didn't realize all the challenges. We never thought about doing any kind of financial projections. If we had gone through a planning process, it would have helped us address all the areas we never thought about. By doing so, we may well have not made the investment, but if we did, we would have been far better able to make the business work for us.

The Principle in Practice

A business plan is all about helping you take your business where you want it to go. If it's going to grow and thrive long-term, there has to be a plan for that growth. You can't just wing it!

In the early stages of a business, you have all kinds of ideas running around in your head. A plan helps focus those ideas. It gives you a start and a direction, allowing you to achieve better results with your financial goals, your competitive advantage, the risks you face, how you plan to market, your day-to-day operations, and areas in which you need help.

As you learn more about your business, and as you adapt to changes in the local business environment, the overall economy, and your own life, you'll find the need for adjustments. And for those who might consider this a waste of time because of that uncertainty, let me remind you what Gen. Eisenhower stated: "In preparing for battle, I've always found that plans are useless, but planning is indispensable."

How Others Have Put This to Work

A number of years ago, about 2010, when I was toying with the idea of using business coaching as an entrepreneurial idea, I volunteered to serve a partnership of three Illinois business owners. They were finalists in an American Farm Bureau Federation's Rural Entrepreneurship Challenge program, which was a national business plan competition, with their idea of a senior move manager business in their community. After writing that plan and following it, their client numbers doubled the next year. They increased their prices by 44 percent, and they tripled their profit margin. Their average job per customer increased by 230 percent. It has continued to serve them well, as they are still in business after fifteen years.

The president, Suzanne, later told me, "We keep coming back [to our business plan] when we have decisions to make. When we seem to get sidetracked, we re-visit what we said we were going to do. We dreamed before writing a business plan; that plan helps us bring those dreams about."

A Question Worth Asking Yourself

To what extent have you planned out your business, your marketing efforts, addressing competition, your operational plans, and long-term financial plans?

_____

_____

_____

_____

_____

_____

The Groundwork Guide™

A lot of business owners start out the way I did, with a great idea, a good work ethic, and some technical skills. The mistake I made, and the one I see far too often, is jumping in without thinking through what it really takes to run the business.

If you're in those early stages, or if you've been running for a while and feel like you're still winging it, I've put together a worksheet to help you. Visit www.RootsandRiversBook.com/FreeTools to download _The Groundwork Guide™_, a simple tool with guiding questions to help you lay a solid foundation. You'll look at what's needed, what could go wrong, and what success will require. While it's not a full-blown business plan, it's a strong first step toward building one.

CHAPTER 2

Decision on Buying the Homeplace

"I am haunted by waters." So ends *A River Runs Through It*, Norman Maclean's gorgeous novella about growing up loving and fishing in the trout streams in his Montana. Reading his words, I get the same sense of belonging to my streams that he so eloquently describes.

The Kentucky River and the Elkhorn Creek are part of my Place. I've loved the history of it. I've loved the setting of the house and the property. Some of my fondest memories are of visiting my Uncle Eddie once he moved back to our homeplace after retiring from his job overseas. We would sit in the backyard watching the river go by, having a scotch and water, just chatting. He was a veteran of the World War II Battle of Okinawa, and he was the only member of his company that was not a casualty. (More on this later.)

Over the years, he'd come to terms with the awful memories, and he could talk about them, and I was fascinated with his stories. He would tell me what he knew about the history of the Place, and he'd relate stories of growing up, both as a young boy in Louisville and as a teenager at the Place on the river. Oddly, his World War II service gave him a taste for travel, and his job gave him an opportunity to see the world, but this was home. While he never said so, I sensed the river and the Place gave him peace. It had the same effect on me when I would visit, and I always felt at home there with him.

Uncle Eddie passed away in November of 2004. The following spring, Francie brought up the idea of moving to the homeplace. Initially, I was excited about the idea, but we quickly realized there were challenges that came with this decision.

The Place had a beautiful setting, and I had a sentimental attachment to the location. The price for the house was reasonable. On the other hand, it was a considerably smaller house than our current home, it was a longer drive to work, and I would have a lot more property to take care of. Being an older home, it was going to be expensive— both fixing it up and living there. And there was the very real issue of potential flooding.

But the chance for me to do some extensive landscaping appealed to me, and I looked forward to the remodeling. I had some skills; I'd done a fair amount of work on my current house, and I felt I had enough background that I could handle all of it. Plus, Dad had done a lot of construction work, and he was excited to help us out.

While there was a lot to consider, the initial conversations Francie and I had were not so much about whether we should do it or not, but rather, how we could make it work. It was where I wanted to be and where I felt we were supposed to be. We had a sense of peace about that. It was where my grandfather and Uncle Eddie spent the last moments of their lives, and it was where I could see myself passing the last moments of my life. I also felt that it satisfied a responsibility to be closer to Mom and Dad as they got older. It was the right call. My youngest daughter got to call it her home, and not just the farm where her grandparents lived. I gained some remodeling skills, and as you'll read later in this book, I developed the closest relationship with my dad that I had ever had. I was there with my parents to help them, which made it easier for me to take on more responsibility with the campground as Dad got older, and I was able to be with my mom in the final moments of her life. All because I came back to my Place.

$$\Diamond$$

I've run into business owners and farmers over the years that were in something of the same position I was, in that they had some sentimentality toward the place they were buying, but they made some choices that were not the best financially. They bought the place with emotion, and used logic to justify it afterwards.

In Sun Tzu's timeless classic, *The Art of War*, there's a quote that says, "Victorious warriors win first and then go to war, while defeated warriors go to war first and then seek to win." Emotion is vitally important in making a decision—it ties into our intuition, our inner sense of whether something is right or not. But in life, and especially in business, we've got to use some logic to make sure our emotions are not getting the best of us.

A long time ago, a farmer told me he made far more money sitting down with a piece of paper and a pencil at his kitchen table than he ever did working in the field with his tractor. The tractor and the fieldwork were vital to make the farm operational, but the thinking and planning done at that table allowed the operational work to mean something. To use a rather grim analogy: The work without the planning is like arranging the deck chairs on the Titanic!

Francie and I made the right call in our move, but sitting down with a piece of paper and writing out the pros and cons of this major life decision would have helped us immensely. It would have given us a better idea of what we were getting into, and we could have planned accordingly for the challenges that confronted us over the next fifteen or so years.

The Principle in Practice

The most important decisions in your life deserve more than just a gut feeling. That instinct matters, but it should be balanced with a clear-eyed look at the facts. A good way to do this is with what is commonly called a SWOT analysis. It's a tool for you to use before you make the decision.

SWOT stands for Strengths, Weaknesses, Opportunities, and Threats. It's a way to step back and look at your business (or any other important life decision) with realism, tempering your natural optimism with some necessary caution.

Strengths and weaknesses are internal factors, like your reputation, experience, capacity, or pricing. Opportunities and threats are external. Opportunities might include market shifts, new customer requests, or partnerships, while threats could be competition, regulations, economic changes, or even burnout.

The real value in this comes from seeing how these factors all connect. This tool will force you to verbalize ideas you haven't completely worked out in your head and confront the potential problems you'd rather ignore. For instance, a strength of yours may open the door to a new opportunity, but a weakness left unaddressed could become a serious threat.

A Question Worth Asking Yourself

What decision are you facing right now that would benefit from a logical pros and cons analysis?

_____

_____

_____

_____

_____

_____

SWOTing Your Decision™

Decisions become more clear when you can see everything laid out in front of you. I've added a tool for you at www.RootsandRiversBook. com/FreeTools, _SWOTing Your Decision_™, a worksheet designed to help you work through some of the biggest and toughest choices with more confidence. It includes guiding questions that will help you find what's working, where you might be vulnerable, and where new possibilities or risks may be hiding.

CHAPTER 3

Living with Floods

I understand flooding. I've lived through it.

I'll never forget that December night in 1978. It had been pouring rain for several days, but a bit of rain doesn't stop a University of Kentucky college student from going to a basketball game against Kansas. It was an exciting game; we won by one point after being down by seven points with thirty seconds left to play so there was some logical celebration afterwards. I got home from that game late and I happened to pick up my roommate's newspaper before I went to bed. A big headline read "Flooding the Worst Ever" in my hometown of Frankfort. My heart sank. My grandparents lived close to the river, and while the water got up in the yard a few times, they had never seen it in the house.

I called my dad, dreading his confirmation. He told me he was meeting a group of people from church to bring them over the hill behind our house on his tractor so they could help Grandmother move out. (The water was already over our entrance road.)

I got there around 1:00 a.m. We took a rowboat within a couple hundred feet of her house, and my dad occasionally went out and moved the boat closer as the water rose. We cut it close. When we finally finished moving all of Grandmother's belongings upstairs, we stepped off her porch and directly into the rowboat.

Because it hadn't happened before, Grandmother was in a state of denial about the flood. She didn't pack anything, and we didn't have anything to pack them into, so we took stacks of dishes and books and piles of clothes and carried them up the stairs.

By the time the next major flood rolled around in 1997, prediction technologies had really advanced—we had a lot more warning that the water would likely get into the house. But old people's attitudes hadn't changed much. Uncle Eddie, about seventy-three at the time, was living in my grandmother's old house, and he was living in as much denial about the flood as Grandmother once had. He also had much more to move than she did, and he didn't pack anything up either. We were able to save everything, but we didn't have time to completely unload all of his bookshelves, so we only moved books from the bottom shelves.

The next day, the river wasn't coming up as fast, but we were still unloading the shelves. I guess it takes a real "river rat" to appreciate this, but while we were moving books upstairs, I actually saw the river crest, meaning it reached its high point and started to recede. On one trip upstairs, I noticed the water was beading up, just getting ready to break over onto the tread of the second step going upstairs. On the next trip, I noticed the water had stopped beading up, and had dropped enough to start showing a fraction of an inch of the nosing on the tread of the step. That was so cool! I actually saw the flood waters crest, which also meant we could stop carrying all these books upstairs!

I took the entire next week off from work and cleaned up Uncle Eddie's house. It was important to start hosing off the walls and floors before the residual mud dried, because it was almost impossible to clean up once it did. I spent all week doing that, and I have *absolutely* no memory of it. I suppose that was my brain's way of putting a terrible job out of my mind.

I learned some lessons from my grandmother and Uncle Eddie. When we moved, I started developing a flood plan. I bought new Lowe's boxes and stored them in the attic of our garage, for the purpose of packing for a flood. In rooms where we replaced some plaster when we remodeled, we used a spray foam insulation that was flood-proof. I developed a list of what needed to be done, in what order, in case we had to move out. I built some tall sawhorses to store basement and garage items on.

Now, the logical question is: After moving my family out of the house two times, who in their *right mind* would ever even consider moving into that house?!

I've been asked that several times over the years. The answer is: It's my home; it's my Place. I've noticed that other people who get flooded out move right back to the same place, and I suppose, like them, the river is in my blood. I've joked that, on average, the water gets in the house every thirty years, so that means we have three days of water, six months of cleanup, and then we get to enjoy the scenery and the serenity of the place for another twenty-nine and a half years!

In the fifteen or so years we lived there, Francie and I had the good fortune of never experiencing water in the house. It got in the unfinished basement a couple of times, but that gave us the chance to try out my flood planning system and make adjustments to it.

$$\Leftrightarrow$$

In 1978 and again in 1997, we were in a rush. The water was fast approaching, and we didn't have time to think—we just *did*. I learned a good lesson then: You need a plan. You need to have a system in place that tells you what to do so the doing becomes a matter of following a well-thought-out set of instructions. Having a system allows you to better prepare for life's uncertainties.

That system needs to be documented. Being the structured, methodical personality that I am, I typed up our flood plans, saved them in an online file, and shared them with the rest of my family. When we moved, I could easily pass on those plans to the new owner of our place.

Any system will need to be adjusted as time goes by. After our basement flooded, we saw that, while our system looked good on paper, there were a few things that weren't as workable in real life.

While we didn't need the system in its entirety, having it gave me peace of mind. I knew I would be ready, even if I dreaded a flood and the resulting work.

The Principle in Practice

As a business owner, if you want to ultimately scale your business, you've got to create systems. It allows the business to take on a life of its own rather than relying solely on what's inside your head.

Michael Gerber, in his book *The E-Myth Revisited*, states it rather plainly: "The purpose of your life is not to serve your business, but the primary purpose of your business is to serve your life."

You're likely proud of what you've created, but this business is not your life. You've chosen it with the hopes it can provide you with the life you want to live, but the paradox is that sometimes, your business gets in the way of your life.

This interference could happen in all kinds of ways. You have the opportunity to take a "bucket list" vacation. You just had a baby and have to take off for a few weeks, or your daughter in another state has a baby and wants you to come and help. Maybe your son or daughter just read this book and is now inspired to buy an old house, and he or she wants your help remodeling it.

Gerber suggests thinking from the standpoint of franchising your business—standardizing everything you do so it can always be done a specific way. There are numerous things in your business you do over and over again, so document those processes.

Create a list of important tasks and develop a flowchart to show the sequence of subtasks that occur within each one. Prioritize what needs to be done first, script out a step-by-step explanation, and have someone do that task based solely on your explanation. From there, you can adjust and clarify as needed.

This will allow you to seize back your life. It's a way to run your business and still have the freedom to do the things that bring you joy.

Another humorous and rather blunt Gerber quote from the same book: "If your business depends on you, you don't own a business, you have a job. And it's the worst job in the world because you're working for a lunatic!"

Don't be that lunatic! Start systemizing your business.

How Others Have Put This to Work

Later in this book, you'll read more about the year I managed my dad's campground and how the systems I implemented led to some conflicts between Dad and me. But as it relates to this topic, systems were a godsend to me.

Dad and I had different management styles. He kept everything in his head, and he wanted to do everything himself. He didn't see the need for this kind of organizational structure.

In contrast, structured systems were vitally important to me, and I used these organizational principles to document the work I did at Dad's campground. The manager had no experience with electronic accounting, so for various bookkeeping jobs, I'd do it once and write it down, show her the step-by-step process, then let her do it while I watched. It worked great because it provided a system in which she could perform those tasks every day, on the spot, and quickly pull up nearly any reports I wanted at a moment's notice.

We also took pictures of minor flood levels and tied them back to the recorded flood stages at the time we took that picture, which gave us a much better planning tool for future flooding predictions.

This documentation of our accounting systems, while it took some time to set up, saved me a great deal of work later in the year, allowing me time to spend on growing the business. And while my dad didn't keep up with the electronic accounting, he did use the pictures we took of the flood levels to help with some decision-making. In fact, it stopped him from having to move out campers one summer, as I'll relate in more detail in Chapter 18.

A Question Worth Asking Yourself

What are the top three things you do that, if someone else could do them, would free up substantial time for you each week, so you could get away from the business to live the life you want?

_____

_____

_____

_____

_____

_____

Essential Task Checklist™

Many business owners stop cold in their tracks when it comes to this task. There's just so much to document, and it's hard to know where to begin. To help you with this, I've put together an *Essential Task Checklist*™, available at www.RootsandRiversBook.com/FreeTools. It's a list of commonly performed tasks, sorted by core function, and it can serve as a foundation for building your own comprehensive manual that outlines how everything is done in your business. It's the start of allowing the business to serve you, rather than the other way around.

CHAPTER 4

Emotional Trauma from Flooding

People in California live under the threat of earthquakes. People in Kansas and Oklahoma are under the gun with tornados. People in Florida expect hurricanes regularly. And people who live along a stream, like me, have to deal with flooding. It's just a fact of life.

For me, a flood wasn't particularly traumatic, but rather just a lot of work, getting ready and cleaning up. (And it wasn't in my house!) I was prepared because I listened to the warnings. My grandmother and Uncle Eddie did not, and they had a much more traumatic experience because of it.

The night we cleaned out Grandmother's house in 1978, she stayed at my parent's home overnight. My mom said Grandmother got up the next morning and looked out the living room window to see her house of forty years sitting in the middle of a flood, its lower portion swallowed up by the water. Mom said she gasped, brought her hand up to her mouth, and started weeping. She couldn't believe what she was seeing.

Each flood is unique. In 1978, the water over our entrance road was rather calm, because it was essentially backwater from the river. In 1997, however, the creek was raging. There had been a lot more rain in the upstream areas of the creek than there was twenty years earlier.

Because of the improved flood prediction models, it looked likely that the water might get into the house again. Uncle Eddie was staying at Mom and Dad's house. My youngest brother, Eric, is mentally handicapped, and being unable to take care of himself, he was there as well. When it looked like the water might also be getting into my parent's house, we didn't have any way to evacuate them from the property.

Dad called the agency responsible for emergency management at the time to see about getting them out. These agency folks wanted to come in a boat across the creek to get them, but my dad was adamantly against it. I was in the house at that moment and heard his side of the phone call. He said he'd lived by that creek all his life, and he had never seen the creek rolling so hard. There was "no way in hell" he was going to let his handicapped son get out on that creek the way it was rolling, especially with someone who didn't necessarily know how to maneuver a boat in flood waters.

Ultimately, it worked. The National Guard sent a rescue helicopter that night, and Uncle Eddie and Eric boarded the helicopter. It took them to the hospital landing pad in the little town where I lived at the time, and Francie picked them up and took them to our house, where they stayed for the next week.

This was nearly thirty years ago, and I still vividly remember my ominous excitement as that rescue helicopter landed on our property, on one of the few high points that wasn't flooded yet. The bright rescue lights shone in the middle of the night, and the wind from the helicopter blades aggressively churned up the water nearby. I still get cold chills from that memory!

Mom never said much about it, and I never had the presence of mind to think to ask, but I can hardly imagine the emotional trauma she felt watching as her husband helped a soldier take her confused, dependent son away from her. She stood by, bundled up in that cold March night—made colder by the helicopter's turbulent winds—knowing she couldn't follow him because she needed to stay back and help those of us who were still moving her out of her own home.

Luckily, the water did not get in Mom and Dad's house. But Dad, as well as my brother Kevin and I, experienced emotional trauma from the flood in a different way.

The bridge over the creek on the entrance road to our property was built sometime in the 1880s. It was a metal truss bridge, and it had a lot of character about it. It added a sense of charm and history to the place, and it was fairly close to the water—enough so that it got flooded pretty regularly, probably once every six to eight years.

I distinctly remember when I was in second grade, the water was quickly coming up from heavy rains, and the county let out school early. I rode home on the bus, got off at the main road, and walked to our house, having to cross that bridge over the creek. My bus driver, Mr. Herbert Perkins, let me off the bus, and waited there on the road until I had safely crossed the bridge walking home. I probably recall it because a classmate told me later that Mr. Perkins said, "He's a brave boy, crossing that bridge all by himself." That feels like a pretty heady thing for someone to say about you when you're in second grade!

When the water was coming up, we typically took the car out to the main road and boated across the creek if we needed to go somewhere before the water went down. It was no big deal. I recall numerous times taking a boat across the bridge instead of a car. Once, I remember us even having to duck our heads to keep from hitting the metal beams on the top of the bridge.

That's just what we did. It's what my dad had done since he was six years old. The bridge had been there all his life, and fifty more years before he got there. It had *always* been there, and we just assumed it always would be there.

As I mentioned, the creek was rolling hard. Somewhere upstream, someone lost a barn. The water lifted that barn off its foundation and carried it downstream. That barn hit our 110-year-old bridge. It took our bridge off its foundation, twisting it up like it was a wrung-out towel, and carried it downstream. Just like that, our bridge was gone.

Dad took the loss of that bridge hard at the time, and so did Kevin and I. That bridge had been there all our lives.

Kevin dealt with the emotions of losing the bridge by writing a poem (below) about it a number of years ago.

When it suddenly got washed away, not only did it shake Dad's emotional foundations—it caused a business crisis as well.

We had an alternate way into the property. The bridge was part of the main road from Frankfort to Cincinnati, until a new road was built by the CCC in the 1930s. The original road was one lane, up against a steep hillside, and hadn't been maintained for fifty years. It was really nothing more than a wide path, so for two to three years, that wide path nearly half a mile long was the only entrance to the property and to my dad's campground. Campers pulling big RV's had to come around this narrow road that was almost impossible to pass on, making it a real hardship. Consequently, a lot of campers quit coming, which made it a severe economic detriment to Dad's campground business.

It took a couple of years, but the county finally built a new bridge that is flood-proof and high enough in elevation that flood waters can't reach it. But that small, common, featureless concrete bridge sure doesn't have the class that our old bridge did.

"Bridges"

Streams: patient and timeless sculptors of earth;
Curious and antiquated means of travel;
Obstinate obstacles to overland commerce;
Destructive forces while lives unravel.

Rivulets, brooks, creeks, and rivers,
Offer aesthetic and geographic comfort, a metaphor
For the need of variety in our existence, solace
From monotony, a boost to help a spirit soar.

The Elkhorn, a stream fork-ed, draining and carrying
Fertile soil that grew tall tobacco and fast horses,
And sprouting little towns and mills, like peas
Perched on its tines, along its courses.

On the upper reaches, places named Little Georgetown,
Bryan Station, Great Crossing and Zion Hill,
Then Switzer, Faywood, big Georgetown and,
Down on the handle, Forks of Elkhorn and Peaks Mill.

A bridge from the past, over this Elkhorn, looking like a
Frustrated stepladder; called a through Pratt truss, replete
With a lattice of riveted steel, perched on a foundation of cut
stone.
The Pratt truss with its wood and steel and stone is now obsolete.

It's a wonder the creek didn't fill up
With the plunging rocks we would drop
From its heights, with wounds only to my pride as
Someone braver than I climbed to its top.

For many years it was a sad bridge,
A wounded bridge, as it suffered from neglect.
And I was despairing as its floor crumbled into the creek,
But, for a while longer, it regained some respect.

As tragedies go, it was minor. This bridge,
My bridge, fell victim to a flood-borne barn filled with hay.
As losses go, it was overwhelming. Alive with so many memories,
I feel its loss as that of a friend to this day.

This willing bearer of 130 years' feet, hooves, wheels, and cargo,
Lying twisted in the receding flood muck,
Was as broken and pitiful as a favorite dog
Run down by a young neighbor's speeding truck.

There's a new bridge now, a monument to efficiency,
To modernism. The only thing is that it lacks a soul.
A pamphlet of equations, a surveyor's benchmark,
The loss of more trees, and then it is done, it is almost whole.

Its cold concrete declares there's no need for respect
For the lives who have crossed over these waters,
No reverence for the stream that has shaped
The lives of this valley's sons and daughters.

I cannot abide Solomon's wisdom, cannot avoid
The question, Why were the old days better than these?
The lack of wisdom in that asking dims
Compared to the foolishness one nowadays sees.

Time will tell that what historians record
Will not ratify the virtues of my memories.
Reflections affirm that my experience as an adult
Makes me long for the return of childhood mysteries

Which now flood into my consciousness as if from a dream,
Building a new bridge from the past to the present,
One structured from love, respect and hope,
Relieving me from a melancholy descent
To wade a stream of despair.

© Kevin L. Strohmeier, 2011

⬖

We all have our own assumptions, our own mental filters through which we see the world around us. They're often based on our past experiences, and they shape our expectations and decision-making, to the point that we limit our possibilities and ignore logic. They can also affect our emotional responses to certain events. But it's important to recognize that our mental filter does not always reflect reality.

Logically, my grandmother knew there was a possibility of floodwaters getting into her house, but she had lived there for forty years and had never seen it happen, so she assumed it never would. Her assumptions caused her to deny the reality, which led to a lack of physical preparation that greatly increased our work on that cold, wet December night in 1978.

My dad assumed the bridge would always be there, so when it no longer was, he took it hard. It caught him by surprise, and he didn't have a plan in place to offset the loss of the bridge. He also wasn't prepared for how this would affect his business.

Every business model is based on underlying assumptions—ones that, if they're wrong, mean you're out of business. If you want to increase your chances of long-term success, you need to address these assumptions.

In the life of a business, there are always going to be unforeseen challenges. If you make the effort to try and identify what might go wrong, you can develop a plan on how to pivot when those challenges arise. Because you have a plan in place on how to shift operations, you stand a much greater chance of weathering that storm.

The Principle in Practice

Most common business metrics don't uncover the assumptions hiding behind your decisions. An assumption is something you take for granted, often without even realizing it. And you cannot measure what you're not aware of.

The key to testing these assumptions is to become aware of how things happen in every part of your business.

To help with this, consider these two questions: "Why do we do it this way?" and "What would happen if . . .?"

Start with your key people. Why do you depend on them? What would happen if they left or could not work for a while?

Move on to your industry practices and your typical way of doing things. Why do you do it this way? What would happen if you tried a different approach?

Now, review your past decisions. If you were starting over, why would you keep doing the things you do, and what would happen if you did it in another way?

As you map out all your major processes, ask these questions at every step. Do the same with your business model, your customers, your marketing and sales strategies, and even those things you've chosen not to do.

Don't do this alone. Customers, employees, or mentors may have some insight that you cannot see.

This can be a very eye-opening experience. It can help you identify things like those bridges that might be washed away so you can be ready with a backup plan. It might even change your entire way of doing things.

A Question Worth Asking Yourself

What are some underlying assumptions about your business that, if they proved to be wrong, could put you out of business?

_____

_____

_____

_____

_____

_____

Business Blindspot Breakdown™

Your hidden assumptions—let's call them blindspots—quietly steer decisions and shape outcomes. They can silently threaten your success, leaving you vulnerable to unexpected setbacks or even business failure.

The *Business Blindspot Breakdown*™ is designed to expose those hidden assumptions. It forces you to think through these beliefs and confront them before they become costly mistakes.

Visit www.RootsandRiversBook.com/FreeTools to download it, and use this tool to challenge what you think you know. It'll help you identify these risky assumptions. The future of your business could depend on it.

CHAPTER 5

Uncle Eddie and Pearl Harbor

It was a visit to the movie theatre Uncle Eddie never forgot. One Sunday, a few years after my grandparents moved to the fishing camp, the family went to see a movie after church. Partway through, someone stopped the film, walked out onto the stage, and announced that the Japanese had just bombed an American military base on an island out in the middle of the Pacific Ocean. They'd never heard of this place called Pearl Harbor before, and the news was sketchy, but it sounded serious. Enough so that the movie was not continued, and everyone in the theatre quietly got up and left their seats, absorbed in their own thoughts.

My Uncle Eddie was a seventeen-year-old high school student on that momentous afternoon. Many years later, as I sat down on one of my visits with him, he (somewhat sheepishly) told me that when he left the theatre that afternoon, all he could think about was how this was going to change his own life.

And it did. Drastically. Uncle Eddie was thirteen when he and his family moved to our homeplace on the river in 1938. He'd grown up in Louisville. His Grandpa Trautwein had built a house in the late 1920s for my grandparents, right next door to Grandpa Trautwein's house, but they lost their new home in the early years of the Great Depression. Uncle Eddie and his family had to move in with his grandparents when he was seven or eight years old, not old enough to recall details, but old enough to remember having a sense of tragedy and being uprooted. He said he remembered his mother looking out the window and bursting into tears when she saw another family walking around in her "beautiful home."

When they moved, Uncle Eddie was of the age that he was an important part of the labor force at the fishing camp and the hotel on the property. He bussed tables at the hotel dining room, he cleaned cabins, and he cut grass across the whole property with a non-motorized push reel mower. He was just an ordinary boy working at his parent's rural business. But in our conversations, I picked up pretty quickly that he realized he didn't want to do that the rest of his life.

He finished high school, joined the Navy, went to boot camp, and shipped out to Guadalcanal, where he trained for what would become the invasion of Okinawa. Serving as a medic in a Marine Raiders unit, he was in the thick of some of the most horrendous fighting in the war.

Millions of World War II veterans lived their entire lives with memories of those awful months and years. Many carried a prejudice against the Japanese their whole lives because of it, but Uncle Eddie was different: The war gave him a taste of different cultures, and he was fascinated. It changed him immensely.

After the war, Uncle Eddie went to college and graduated with an art degree. He soon had the opportunity to become a civilian employee with the Army in occupied Japan. He came to love and appreciate the people and the culture. He started collecting Far Eastern ancient art, and continued that collection his entire life. He traveled across Asia while he lived in Japan. About six years later, he transferred to an Army base near Nuremberg, Germany, and lived there almost twenty years, widely traveling through Europe and Africa while he was there.

But when all was said and done, he retired and returned home, to his Place on the river, where I really got to know him and spend time enjoying the peace of the river with him.

$$\diamondsuit$$

We are all going to experience things in our life that will shake our world. It might be world events like the bombing of Pearl Harbor, a terrorist attack, or a COVID-19 outbreak. It might be a regional event like a massive flood or a devastating tornado.

It might be an unforeseen local event that impacts your business in a drastic way, like the unexpected arrival of a big competitor, or the biggest local employer moving somewhere else, or a supply chain disruption, or a permanent road or bridge closure, or even a family tragedy.

You could argue that the astute business owner should have seen this coming and should have been ready for any kind of risk that comes along. Maybe he or she should have, but the reality is that the vast majority of business owners don't have the time, nor the energy, nor the insight to be able to predict all these possibilities. Most of us will be blindsided.

When this happens, you've got to take the time to process it, and in some cases to grieve over whatever loss this may have entailed. We have to do this for our own emotional and mental well-being, to come to terms with the loss and allow ourselves to adapt to this new reality. Don't be ashamed of how you feel. We all go through it, and the time we take to help us move on is crucial for us.

But then, you've got to shift your mindset. Composer Jerome Kern may have said it best: "You've got to pick yourself up, dust yourself off, and start all over again." Instead of looking at what you've lost, focus on what opportunities might be presented by this new, unforeseen challenge.

Here are some examples:

- Some restaurants went under during COVID, but some figured out ways to serve their patrons outdoors or started providing take-out or delivery.

- A ski resort diversified its offerings with hiking trails, wine tastings, and live music events in response to some abnormally warm weather.

- A bridge closing forced a business to move to a new location to better serve its customers.

- A state government office closed downtown, taking away hundreds of downtown employees and causing several downtown businesses to drastically adjust their marketing efforts.

- A liquor store located on the county line of a "dry" county, in order to provide service to those county residents, changed over to become a nightclub when that dry county voted to allow alcohol sales.

Making these kinds of changes requires a new way of thinking, but the business owner that is able to quickly adapt to a new reality in their world is more likely to find new ways to be successful.

The Principle in Practice

It's not easy to make these big adaptations, but the payoff can be huge. My Uncle Eddie's nervousness ultimately led to a fulfilled life of travel and adventure. You've got to start by recognizing that what you are about to do is new, and consequently, there's going to be some uncertainty. Try to get comfortable with a little ambiguity.

Any major change comes with risks, but it also brings possibilities. The key is to reframe the situation. You've got this challenge; how can you make it have a positive impact on your business? How can you turn this into a new, unexplored goldmine? As you focus on the possibilities, look at what you and your business need to do better. Look at the skills, attitudes, and perspectives you'll need to learn and embrace.

That's the emotional aspect of how to move forward. Now step into the logical, investigative side of opportunity assessment.

Try to objectively analyze what has happened and pinpoint the true scope of what this currently means to your existing business. Often, the situation is not as dire as it first appears. Even if it is, don't stop!

You've been given this occasion to rethink, so take a close look at the chances for innovation.

Review what your current strengths are. What is it that you do best, and why is that so? How might you be able to re-purpose those strengths?

Take a look at how your competitors might react to this outside shake-up of the business landscape. How might you step in and do it better than them? How might it create possibilities for strategic partnerships that can open new doors for you?

Forced transitions are hard, and they can shake you and your business, but if you lean into it, it might be the opening that takes your business in an exciting new direction.

A Question Worth Asking Yourself

What are ten unthinkable things that, if they happened, could derail your business? For each of those ten things, reframe that cost as an opportunity.

_____

_____

_____

_____

_____

_____

The Unthinkable Reframer™

Most of us don't plan for the unthinkable until it happens. Taking the time now to imagine what could go wrong can help you find out what might go right. *The Unthinkable Reframer™* is a tool designed to help you identify potential unexpected events that could shake your business and guide you in reframing each one into a possible path forward.

Visit www.RootsandRiversBook.com/FreeTools to download this worksheet. It can help you step back and see how disruption does not have to mean devastation. When you look at it from another point of view, you might even find that disruption holds the seed of something new—something better.

CHAPTER 6

Sugar Rationing at the Hotel

When my grandparents bought the fishing camp in rural Franklin County in 1938, they were buying more than just a fishing camp.

The property was owned by Lonnie and Americus Quire, who bought the place in 1919. It had been the shipping point for farmers in the area for many years, and it had a ramp down to the river, a cabin that served as an office, and a silo to store feed for livestock. The Quires had a vision, and they developed not only a fishing camp but a resort area, complete with several rental cabins. In about 1923, they added a hotel onto the property.

This three-story hotel rented out rooms on the weekends. Guests stayed on the second and third floors, and the first floor was the designated dining hall, where they served their famous chicken dinners—by reservation only.

Mr. Quire was not someone easily impressed. One time, in the early 1930s, a car pulled up in front of the hotel and a couple men got out and asked for a table. Mr. Quire asked if they had reservations, and they said no. He told them if they didn't have reservations, he couldn't seat them. These two gentlemen said, "I don't think you know who we are. Governor Laffoon (the Kentucky governor from 1932–1935) is in the car, and he'd like to eat here." Mr. Quire told them, "I don't care who's in the car. If you don't have reservations, you don't eat!" So the Governor and his entourage turned around and left, without getting the chicken dinner they so desired.

As I mentioned earlier, my Uncle Eddie bussed tables at the hotel. My Aunt Ginny and my dad also carried out meals to people and cleaned up tables. It was truly a family operation.

World War II changed things, in ways that a lot of people today don't realize. The government implemented rationing of various goods in order to manage the shortages of consumer goods caused by the massive war efforts. This originally applied to food items like coffee, butter, and canned goods, with sugar being the first item rationed in the summer of 1942, but it soon included non-food items like gasoline and tires.

Businesses like my grandparents' hotel struggled with this rationing. Individual households came first, and my grandparents weren't able to get enough of the food items they needed to provide the meals they used to. People also weren't able to travel the way they used to. This once-attractive retreat, located far out in a rural community, soon became a luxury visitors couldn't afford.

People still came to the camp for a weekend, but my grandparents weren't able to sustain the day traffic they needed to maintain the dining room, so they closed the hotel part of the business.

After the war ended, they considered re-opening, but the cabin and boat rental for fishermen was profitable enough that they decided against it. Plus, two of their kids were off at college, with my dad being the only one left at home. He'd gotten involved in playing basketball, and had started a substantial cattle operation for a teenager, so they'd lost a considerable portion of their labor force. They found that life was a lot less stressful without the efforts required to keep the busy dining hall open. Instead, they turned part of the first floor into apartments, renting them out to fishermen on the weekends, and used the rest of the hotel for storage.

Over time, with most of the building serving no useful purpose, my family had no reason to keep up maintenance, and the place fell into disrepair. But with that neglect, that old hotel provided a vast world of exploration opportunities for Kevin and me. Growing up, we loved to go to the upstairs rooms and see what kind of treasures we could find, the leaky rooms and fallen plaster fueling our imaginations.

In 1987, Uncle Eddie finally tore the place down. The crumbling building was too far gone for a reasonable remodel, and it made logical sense to get rid of it, but I still hated to see it go.

$$\Leftrightarrow$$

I don't know if my grandparents saw this coming and stayed ahead of it, or if it was solely a reaction to world events. I do know this hurdle changed the way they operated, and it was apparently successful, as their modified business structure continued for decades.

Any business around for any length of time will face challenges beyond your control. It might be changes brought on by world events, such as what I just described, or it can involve other things like demographic shifts brought about by larger economic policies, differences in generations and how they think, technological advances, evolution in consumer attitudes, needs and desires, or specific changes within your industry.

Wayne Gretzky, one of professional hockey's leading scorers, had the ability to anticipate his teammates and his competitor's actions, which allowed him to position himself in the right place, at the right time, to execute the right move. As he said, the trick is to "skate to where the puck's going to be, not where it is." As an entrepreneur, you want to take a similar approach.

The desires and tastes of your customers change over time, and since those customers drive your company's success, you have to make sure what you're offering always aligns with what they want and need.

Keeping track of industry trends not only helps you stay relevant to your customers, it also helps lay the groundwork for competitive analysis. Tracking these trends keeps you ahead of your competitors because most of them aren't putting in the time, nor the effort, to do it themselves.

The Principle in Practice

In the early 1990s, I, along with three co-workers, developed a management training program for farmers in our area. Like any good speakers, we wanted to quickly grab people's attention, so we started with a discussion on agricultural megatrends that were published by an Iowa State economist named Neil Harl. I won't go into the details, because the trends themselves aren't important here, but it did generate some lively discussion, as most of the audience didn't see any way these things could happen. Some thirty-five years later, they've ALL come to pass.

Dr. Harl patterned his discussion after John Naisbitt's groundbreaking book, *Megatrends*. Naisbitt emphasized, "The most reliable way to forecast the future is to try to understand the present." By carefully observing the small shifts happening around us today, we can begin to see the larger transformations that are coming. What these shifts suggest about the future, we can use to shape our own future.

Join trade associations to get their publications and to keep up with what the experts within your industry are saying. Ads in these trade publications can give you a hint of consumer trends. Look for not only what is happening, but try to discern the why behind it.

Find some websites or podcasts sites related to what you do and compare them to other similarly-themed sites. If a trend is emerging, people will be talking about it. Follow what others are saying to help you capitalize on it.

Making network connections also allows you to take advantage of a wider variety of resources and insights that could prove useful. In the context of business trends, people within your network may be able to point out trends in your industry in their initial stages. This will allow you to get in on something early and benefit from it as much as possible in the long run.

Look at what the leading companies in your industry are doing. They're in their positions, in part, because they jump on trends before anyone else. If you're paying attention, you may begin to notice newly adopted practices that are keeping those companies ahead of the game.

Finally, gather information about your customers. Try sending out surveys, providing polls through social media, or conducting market research that will offer insight into the behavior of people who buy from you.

A Question Worth Asking Yourself

What industry or consumer trends are going on right now that could affect the way you do business?

_____

_____

_____

_____

_____

_____

The Trend Navigator™

Staying ahead means having a sense of what's coming next. _The Trend Navigator_™ helps you spot emerging industry and customer trends before they become obvious. Visit www.RootsandRiversBook.com/FreeTools to download this worksheet. With guiding questions and space to capture insights, it's a simple way to track changes that could impact your business so you can adapt early and position yourself for success.

How Others Have Put This to Work

A Missouri IT service provider had a good business, but he began to realize he was doing it all. J. R.'s team deferred to him on nearly every decision, customers wanted him, not an employee, and he was working sixty-five to seventy hours a week. The business completely owned him.

Through an extensive strategic planning process, he started making some changes. After a careful SWOT analysis, he realized his communication with his team was a severe weakness. I helped him improve his system of weekly meetings, which consisted of him telling his team what to do every week, and shifted the focus to tracking metrics and reviewing goals. Over time, these employees took on responsibilities he never would have imagined. They helped him develop his first Strategic Plan, and he said, "They've gone further with it than I ever even thought of myself. It's exciting, but it's also scaring me to death what they think we can do with this business." A year ago, he couldn't even be gone for a day without the place falling apart!

He had a gnawing fear in the back of his mind that the company had no safety net if he couldn't work. "What would happen to my business if I had a car wreck?" he asked, and we addressed those questions of risk to his satisfaction. He now says, "We've now got procedures built to run this business without me. I don't worry about that anymore."

Through an industry trends study, he saw the possibilities of setting himself apart through AI automation. It was a game-changer. He went from closing an average of twenty-five tickets a week to about 550 a week, with most of them requiring no manual work. This has all been fueled by setting systems in place.

The result of all these changes? In the last two years, receipts have increased by 60 percent, and his net profits in the first five months of this year have increased by a whopping 590 percent from the same time last year. He's also gotten his life back. He now works forty hours a week, and he plays golf most Fridays. He told me, "I don't have bad days anymore. I have good days and great days." And maybe one the best compliments he paid to me: "You've helped me build a business that's fun!"

PRINCIPLE TWO

Leverage Your Livelihood

*The Ways in Which the Money
Comes into the Business*

"Build it, and they will come." A great line in a great movie (*Field of Dreams*). What's not to like about it? It's got baseball. It's got Kevin Costner in a sports movie. It's got baseball. It's got James Earl Jones's deep, resonant, authoritative voice. It's got baseball.

But when it comes to building a business, that great line is not very good advice.

There may have been a time when having a great product was sufficient for a business to succeed, but not anymore. That great product is only a starting point. Your prospects, even your loyal customers, are bombarded with choices every day. With all that noise and distraction, you need more than just a quality product to stand out. You need a clear offer.

My father-in-law's hobby was Model T's. He was always tinkering around with them, from the moment I met him. There were two, named Lizzie and Tex, that he'd drive around his small town on the weekend afternoons, getting a big kick out of waving and honking the horn at the kids who were out in their yards.

He and his wife enjoyed going to antique car shows. He'd talk to the exhibitors, admire the body work, look under the hood, and genuinely seem to enjoy his time there. At least that's what I thought he did. When I mentioned something about it, I found out it was not all fun and relaxation. He said something to the effect of "I'm seeing what they did, so I can do it better!"

He was investigating his competition. When you approach it with the right mindset, like my father-in-law did, this research doesn't have to be hard.

In this section, I'll address several important topics: You need to know who you're after, who else is after them, how to entice them to do business with you, and how to ensure they continue doing business with you.

It's vital to know who will be most interested in your product or service. You do this for two reasons: First, marketing is too expensive to throw some kind of advertising out there for everyone to see; no matter what you sell, only a select few will be even remotely interested in it. Second, by focusing on a select market, you can better determine what they're truly interested in and refine your marketing message to more closely resonate with customers' wants and desires. To continue our baseball analogy, a good hitter doesn't swing at every pitch. They wait for just the right ones in their strike zone, the ones they can actually hit well. In business, your strike zone is your target client. If you chase every lead or try to appeal to everyone, you waste energy and strike out more often.

Once you know who it is you're serving, you need to understand who else is after that same customer dollar. Knowing your competition and understanding where you fit in is crucial. In order to show your customer you're the best choice, you need to know what all their options are. It may even mean you need to refine your marketing message to focus on what they *aren't* getting elsewhere. Taking our baseball analogy a step further, baseball teams spend hours studying their opponents—the strengths of the likely pitchers, where hitters tend to swing, and who struggles under pressure.

Your profit results from a combination of these factors, all of which work together to bring in more leads, convert those leads into paying customers, keep them coming back, increase the average amount they spend with you, and protect your margins. This requires a variety of creative and consistent efforts on your part.

In this manner, running a successful business is like regularly winning at baseball. You can't rely on one power hitter or amazing pitcher to carry you through. Not only do you need home runs, you need good consistent base hitters, you need solid relief pitching, you need smart base running, and you need good fielding. If any one area is weak, then the whole team suffers.

CHAPTER 7

Pricing of Campground Services

As my dad aged and spent more time taking care of my ailing mother, I offered to help him with the management of his business. He's not one to accept help, but he agreed I could assist him with some things. Having studied business management principles for the last several years, I felt I was well-equipped for the job.

I soon realized we had different visions. He thought I could cut grass, which we had a LOT of on the property. While he had a couple campers who helped out occasionally, and it was something he enjoyed doing, it could quickly get ahead of him. I wanted to assist him in areas in which I had expertise; I wasn't interested in just being a non-paid hired hand.

When he finally agreed to let me put my knowledge to use, I spent several weeks visiting other campgrounds around us to find out what they were doing and how we compared to them.

In some cases, I made appointments and met with the owners on my visit. Other times, I just happened by, anonymously picking up brochures, checking out the campstore and showerhouse, and getting a general feel of the place.

Because of this, I discovered our bathroom facilities were not on par with other campgrounds and that we lacked the popular feature of a playground on our property, but I confirmed we had the best stream access of any other place in the region. We also had the largest sites around, which was intentional on Dad's part, based on campgrounds he'd visited thirty years previously, and we allowed more flexibility with our permanent campers building elaborate decks.

When I also learned my dad's prices were the lowest a private campground offered in all of central Kentucky, I put together a proposal that brought our camping rates up to about the average of the region. I included a grandfather clause for current campers that raised it in small increments over three years but still stayed lower than new campers. I thought I had done well.

Dad didn't buy it. He didn't want prices that high; he worried some of his clientele couldn't afford the higher rates. He also thought it would be confusing to have different camping rates for existing and new campers, so nothing changed.

As I mentioned before, I sensed an inkling of difference between what the two of us envisioned the campground to be. Dad had become involved volunteering at the homeless shelter over the years, and his vision of the campground had evolved toward providing a home for the homeless. He wanted it to be affordable for his target customers.

I looked at this campground as more of a recreational getaway for families who valued water sports. With our large sites, I felt we could easily charge considerably more than average, though I didn't think that was appropriate at the time; a nice showerhouse was highly valued, and ours was in a low floodplain, designed for quick cleanouts (it flooded, on average, every five to seven years). In thirty years, it was really showing its age, and Dad wasn't interested in making the substantial investment for an upgrade.

But now that I'd learned what other campgrounds offered and what our customers wanted us to provide, I had a better grasp on our strengths and weaknesses. While I wasn't able to implement any changes to the campground at that time, my research wasn't a waste. In fact, I used it to increase weekend prices several years later when I took over management of the place.

$$\Leftrightarrow$$

Nearly every owner of other campgrounds I met with on my visits was really tied down to their business during the camping season, my dad included, because they all valued being involved in the everyday actions.

It took time, and I needed to be tactful when I spoke, but this research of our competition wasn't all that hard. The owners were generally happy to talk to someone in their same industry, and they were proud of what they'd done, even sharing with me the challenges they'd had along the way.

I learned valuable lessons from them, one being that pricing matters. As a general rule, the higher the prices, the more well-kept the campground.

I also got a strong sense as to what campers were looking for. At destination campgrounds like ours (compared to transient campgrounds, where the camper just passes through), people were looking for a community. We did that well.

The Principle in Practice

Every business has competition. Knowing what your competitors are doing will allow you to find and take advantage of opportunities as they arise.

Marla Tabaka, a regular contributor to *Inc.* magazine, owned a coffee shop outside of Chicago. In one of her *Inc.* articles, she said a business should stop viewing its competition as the enemy, but rather use it as a "catalyst to brilliance." She recognized she couldn't compete with the nearby Starbucks, so she didn't try. Instead, she looked for areas to excel where Starbucks did not, because she believed envying your competitors wasted energy that could be better used to help you become the best entrepreneur you can be.

A systematic approach to competition research that goes beyond a casual knowledge allows you to better understand where you shine and how you can capitalize on that. It also gives you a sense of how a competitor might react to something you do. Most importantly, knowing what your competitors are offering gives you a better understanding of what your customer really desires.

As you go about this research, you'll want to find out the basic, easily accessed information, like prices, products and services offered, and promotions, but you'll also want to dig deep and determine why customers buy from them and what internal operational factors cause this business to behave as it does.

See how they handle their sales and treat their customers. Go to their website and social media pages, look at their online reviews, and look for any ads they may be running. If you can, talk to their previous customers and find out why they purchased from that business. As you do this, write down what you learn and observe.

Once you do that, compare yourself with them. Determine where each of you stand out, looking at it from both a customer's point of view, as well as what you can determine to be their internal operational strengths.

Hopefully, you'll find you stand out in at least a few areas, so you can determine how to use those advantages.

Knowing your competitors is a competitive advantage in itself!

How Others Have Put This to Work

Studying the competition has helped me understand where I bring something different to the table in my own business. In networking meetings over the years, I've noticed many business coaches come from specialized backgrounds—accounting, behavioral science, or corporate leadership. These are valuable paths, but they're different from mine.

I've come to understand what sets me apart is the perspective that comes from owning and managing a business myself. I've lived with the pressure of making payroll, trying to determine the appropriate inventory, worrying about marketing that didn't work, juggling too many roles, and wondering what to do next. That lived experience gives me a deep understanding of what small business owners face, far more than theory or credentials can provide.

In that same research, I also began to see another pattern. Many coaches focus on isolated areas, such as marketing, finance, team building, often depending on their own professional background. Not many offer a structured, whole-business system. This gap is where I've found my footing.

Over the past twenty years, I've developed a framework that helps business owners build a structure strong enough to support growth. That system has been shaped by international training, national coaching experience, and the work of writing a business planning book, *The Indispensable Start,* which has since been used as a college text. More than that, it's been shaped by two decades of experience working in the trenches with real entrepreneurs.

My approach is holistic and real to the life of a business owner, their goals, their energy, and their wants and dreams. I believe the business should serve the owner, not the other way around. My whole coaching system flows from that belief.

A Question Worth Asking Yourself

Think of your most logical competitor. What do they do better than you, and what do you do better than they do? How do those strengths cater to what your customers actually want?

_____

_____

_____

_____

_____

_____

The Competitor Detective™

Understanding your competition goes beyond just knowing their prices and products. *The Competitor Detective*™ worksheet helps you dig deeper into what your competitors do well, where you stand out, and how you can use those insights to sharpen your own business advantage.

Visit www.RootsandRiversBook.com/FreeTools to download this simple, straightforward tool so you can rise above the competition and shine where it matters the most.

CHAPTER 8

Moonlight Floats

My grandmother had a collection of old '78 records she loved, and when I was a kid, I had a little portable record player I'd take over to her house. One of her favorites was a song by the Mills Brothers. I can still hum its tune and recall the lyrics: "Oh, the moonlight's fair tonight along the Wabash . . ." It's a romantic song about a river—what could be more appealing?

I suspect I remember it so well, in part, because one of my relatives had a cabin on the Wabash River in Southern Indiana, but also because my experiences on the river allowed me to personally connect with the song.

The folks who owned the canoe livery I visited on the Licking River came up with the idea of a moonlight canoe trip. On certain weekends, they launched a guided paddle trip down the stream, with the full moon providing the light to see your way downstream. I went once, and I remember humming this "On Banks of the Wabash" tune as I maneuvered the riffles in the imperfect light, which was hard to do.

I thought about my wider Kentucky River with no riffles, and I saw an opportunity to improve on their idea.

Francie and I prepared for our own Moonlight Float launch by taking a couple trips on our own to make sure the time and the moonlight worked out the way we wanted. From our put-in point upstream that we called Tillet's Landing, it was about a two-hour trip. We launched at dusk, and as we paddled north, the moon began to peek through the trees along the east bank of a large bottom-land field. When the river meandered, turning east, that bank became a large cliff. We could no longer see the moon in those moments, but we still got the benefit of its light. Further downstream, the river turned north again, and as we paddled, suddenly the moon appeared high above the cliff, in all its glory, and we completed the trip in its full light. It was absolutely beautiful.

Francie and I planned to lead the trip in the front canoe, with my dad bringing up the rear, making sure no one fell behind. When we got to our take-out point, which was my dad's launch ramp, he would come in and start a big bonfire, Francie and I would help everyone out of their canoes, and we would finish the trip with everyone roasting hot dogs over the fire.

But we did something different with our inaugural trip. We wanted to make it special, so we created a nice restaurant scene. I pulled my car up near the picnic tables and played classical music on the cassette tape deck. We sat our first-time customers along the river at tables set with calligraphied name tents and placemats. My mother prepared a number of dishes we could serve in an outdoor setting (with no available electricity), and she, along with Francie and me, personally delivered the meals to each table.

I'd advertised the evening through local canoe groups, and I'd also called friends who lived in the neighboring county, where I worked my full-time job. That method of promotion worked; we rented out all of our canoes. There wasn't a cloud in the sky that evening, and the moon did not disappoint!

We wanted to do this up right to make it a memorable experience for all, but there was a problem, one that has stuck in my mind over the years: Through the course of the evening, various people hollered at me, asking me to "turn down that awful music." After a while, I did, but I recall being really put out that these people, who were attending a nice, well-done event, could be so rude. We were proud of the atmosphere we'd tried to present, and it bothered me that some of my acquaintances didn't appreciate what we were providing.

It wasn't just me who was annoyed. Several people came up to me as they were leaving to say they'd enjoyed what we'd done, and they apologized for their fellow customers' catcalls about the music.

Maybe I should have played the Mills Brothers . . .

$$\Leftrightarrow$$

I understand now it wasn't their fault they didn't like my music. It was my fault for either not providing the music my customers wanted, or not looking for customers that appreciated the music we intended to provide.

If a business is going to provide a worthwhile product, service, or experience their customer values, they need to meet that customer where he or she is. It's not the business's job to change the customer's ideas, but rather to provide what the customer already wants and highly regards. If what you provide doesn't fit what your customer wants, you need to adjust your product offering. Or if what you offer is something that uniquely fits your core competency, you may need to adjust your marketing so you find the customers that want what you provide.

In order to do this, in order to know if you're meeting the desires of that customer, you've got to get to know them. You need a thorough understanding of them—who they are, where they live, what they want, how they behave, and what they can afford. This was something I failed to do in those early days of my own entrepreneurial development, and I still recall the results of that failure.

The Principle in Practice

Many business owners skip over this step, not because they don't have time for it, but because they don't see the need for it. They market to everyone so they don't risk losing out on potential customers.

On the surface, this is entirely logical, but they're only making it harder on themselves to market their product or service. In order to appeal to everyone, the marketing message becomes so broad that it fails to connect with most people. It's like packing for a trip. If you don't know where you're going, you'll have to pack a little of everything, both your winter coat and your swimsuit. If you know your destination, you can pack exactly what's needed and lighten your load considerably.

Focus on attracting the customers you REALLY want. Stop chasing the crowd and get clear on the specific audience you were built to serve. When you focus on your best possible customers and specifically cater to them, they become loyal fans who return often, bring friends, and spread the word, building your business naturally.

To do this, develop a crystal-clear picture of your ideal customer, often called a customer avatar. Start with the people who already love what you do, who buy without you having to convince them, and who come back regularly. Formally describe them, first with basic facts like age, location, work, and income, then dig deeper. How do they spend their days and weekends? Where do they shop? What motivates them? What do they worry about, and what problems are they trying to solve?

You learn this by listening and asking. Pay attention to what they buy and why. Talk to them, run short surveys, ask questions at checkout, and observe patterns. Involve your team; they may notice what you miss. This helps you avoid making assumptions.

One of the best books I've read on this topic is a self-published book titled *Profile Your Target Market* by Scott Gardner. He emphasizes that "you don't create an avatar, you discover it from your real customers, and once you truly know them, you'll be able to clone your best clients."

As you gather insights, create a short, written profile with a name, and maybe an icon, that makes them feel real. Check every marketing piece against that avatar. Over time, you can create more than one, refining as you learn. When you start attracting more of the right people, you'll save money with more effective marketing. By concentrating on your best customers—who will buy more and buy it often—you'll also make money.

A Question Worth Asking Yourself

How do you define your target customer, and how are you truly meeting their needs? How do you know?

_____

_____

_____

_____

_____

Buyer Persona Planner™

Trying to reach as many people as possible leaves you with a message so broad it doesn't connect with anyone. By defining exactly who your best customers are and focusing your efforts toward them, you grow a stronger, more profitable business.

Visit www.RootsandRiversBook.com/FreeTools to download the _Buyer Persona Planner_™ to help you identify the people you best want to serve. It walks you through the process of noticing patterns, asking the right questions, and building a clear profile you can actually use.

CHAPTER 9

Managing the Campground

My house was on the same property as my parents' home, and we only lived a tenth of a mile away from each other. I saw them all the time, so I noticed my dad's escalating stress over the years. I mentioned before that he ran a campground, but he also took care of my mother, who suffered from dementia in the last stages of Parkinson's disease. In his late eighties, it was too much for him, but he refused to even consider anyone's help. He had a sense that no one else would take care of Mom like he could, and I suspect he was right, but the physical stress continued to build. He got sick. Really sick. He had to go to the hospital on Memorial Day weekend, one of the biggest weekends for the campground, where he stayed for several months.

That weekend, it became my responsibility to run his campground. He was so sick that I didn't really expect him to ever come home. If he did, I imagined he would need long-term care. Plus, I wouldn't be able to care for Mom like he did. Whether they stayed home with some live-in care or went to a nursing home, it was going to require a lot of money, which the campground wasn't earning.

Dad was exhausted. While the campground was his pride and joy, the place had fallen into decline because he was too worn out to take care of the place like it needed. People weren't paying their bills, they were letting their sites get junky, and this lack of oversight had allowed for the introduction of drug problems. I felt my responsibility was to fix these problems.

It was a stressful summer. Not only did I have the responsibilities of running the business, I was taking care of Mom and driving to the hospital an hour away, every day, to check on and be with Dad.

Mom's Parkinson's symptoms had been on hold for a number of months. While she suffered some dementia, she knew what was going on with Dad. Shortly after he left for the hospital, she started a rather rapid decline. It might have been that in her mind, she didn't believe Dad would survive. They'd been married for sixty-four years, and I sense that she gave up fighting. Near the end, Dad had improved enough that we were able to get private transportation so he could come home and be with her during her last days. She passed away in mid-August, almost three months after Dad first left for the hospital.

That was the personal stress. Back at the campground, I had uncomfortable changes to make as well. It started with getting rid of some live-in campers who were causing behavioral problems, and dealing with customers who became upset when I actively began to collect past-due bills.

I also began forcing the cleanup of sites from long-term resident campers who had let their campsites get cluttered. Not only was this a marketing problem, as it chased off a lot of good camping prospects, but it made for a lot more work in case of flooding. But it didn't make these offending campers very happy.

While these actions were challenging, we were able to turn a declining business into one that was well on its way to becoming very profitable. We computerized record-keeping and invoicing, which allowed us to begin regular collection of camper fees. We automated a system of determining electric fees, which cut a day-long chore down to less than an hour. We began paying bills on time, and having been the lowest-priced campground within the central Kentucky region, we finally increased our prices for weekend campers to about the regional average.

We upgraded the boat launch and put in a new canoe access, which allowed for new business from boaters and creek enthusiasts. Tubing on the creek was becoming popular, so we devised a system to collect payment from people using our property, which had gone largely uncollected in previous years.

By cleaning up the sites and getting rid of problem campers, we began rebuilding the outside reputation of the campground within the larger community. The sheriff thanked us that he no longer had to make regular trips onto the property at all hours of the night, and two nearby campgrounds began recommending us to their overflow campers.

These improvements showed in the financial health of the business. When I started, the business had over $10,000 of credit card debt. By the end of the year, that was completely paid down. Though I didn't take over management of the place until after the camping season was nearly one-third over, the annual revenues for the business that year increased by over 25 percent compared to the previous year. That business was also recurring, and it continued to grow in future years.

I was proud of what we accomplished. The campground was profitable, bills were being paid, the place looked more well-kept, longer-term plans were being formulated, prices were consistent with the competition, and we had built back up the level of respect in the community it had when Mom and Dad were healthy.

$$\Leftrightarrow$$

Francie and I had a retail storefront business for about eighteen years in a small town near my homeplace. She had a real skill in custom picture framing, and we also took on a retail paint dealership. In those fifteen years, we were able to survive, but we were never profitable enough for us to consider it successful. We eventually made the decision to close the store and sell off the inventory.

We felt like failures. As you've read earlier, I'd been a tobacco farmer for a few years, and I'd owned and operated a canoe livery, so I felt like I knew how to run a business. With our store, we were good at what we did. We provided real quality; we were part of the community, but we just couldn't pull it off.

Along with the store, I had another job as a farm advisor (formally, a county agent) in that same community with the University of Kentucky. Around the same time the store closed, I had the opportunity to be part of a leadership development program designed to help rural Kentucky communities become more entrepreneurial. What I learned was that, like most small business owners, we knew how to *do*; we didn't know how to manage or how to market. I thought at the time, *WHY didn't I know all this while we had the business?!* It would have made life so much easier!

Looking back on it, I think it was God's way of saying, "Buddy, I've got something in mind for you." If our business had been successful right from the beginning, I likely wouldn't have found my calling. With that program, I realized I could help people grow their businesses. I could help them *not* have to struggle like we did and instead find some peace of mind, because their businesses now work for them. I was excited about it.

After that program, I furthered my entrepreneurial education through reading about and researching the best practices in business. Some skills we learned were focused toward a high-tech, gazelle-type business, which was not the businesses we were likely to be working with, so I eventually adapted these materials into a comprehensive business planning book titled *The Indispensable Start*. After I retired from my farm advisor job, I took on a position as a coach with a marketing company, where I further refined my business skills.

It was about fifteen years after that leadership program when the campground became my responsibility. I used the same strategies I had learned to increase those revenues. I had learned that growth comes, first, by generating new leads. We did that, in large part, by developing an active social media presence that hadn't been there before. Plus, the boat and canoe launch helped attract new prospects. When people stopped by to check out the campground, which we had cleaned up significantly, we greatly increased our conversion rates because it was more enticing to prospective campers. We also kept customers coming back by providing a peaceful, quiet setting and getting rid of the night-time troublemakers. By getting rid of those who weren't paying their bills, we generated more average revenue per customer. Increasing our prices also increased our Gross Profit Margin.

There were plenty of other opportunities to increase revenues and profits as well. We didn't lower fixed costs that year, as there were some needed improvement costs and overdue expenses we had to pay, but we set the stage for easier management of expenses through the computerization of our records. Plus, there was plenty of land area available for growth, so we started setting plans in place for an additional twenty to thirty campsites, which were put in two years later.

The Principle in Practice

When most people look at how their business is doing, they look at the overall revenues and their net profit. The problem is, a business owner *does not* control those two numbers. What he or she *does* control are those areas that *lead* to profit.

You don't get new customers, per se. What you do is the work of creating leads and converting those leads, which, in turn, generates new customers.

You have to provide a product or service that is useful to customers and makes them want to spend their dollars with you. You also have to recognize that past customers don't automatically come back. You need to provide the value and the customer experience to entice them back.

Internally, you need to carefully work at making sure that the price for which you're selling the product or service more than covers both the cost of providing the product or service itself *and* the overhead expenses that come from running a business before anything is sold.

Most business owners recognize that all this needs to happen, but they don't think in terms of the specific efforts needed to generate those profits. By thinking in these terms, all they have to do to grow the business is make adjustments in those areas I mentioned: leads, conversion rates, retained customers, average spend per customer, gross profit margin, and fixed costs.

A little-known secret is that small incremental increases in each of these areas can make phenomenal changes in overall profit. These small changes can make 50–75 percent increases in net profit and add tens of thousands of dollars into the business bank account.

Take a look at your own numbers. Calculate how much of a change a 5 or 10 percent improvement in each of these areas would make in your overall profitability. Then identify one action in each area that would bring that growth about.

How Others Have Put This to Work

The owner of a power-washing business was stuck. A solo-preneur, Jose had built a solid website and followed a typical marketing pattern, relying heavily on social media. But he had reached his limit of the hours he could personally work, and the business was barely covering his living expenses.

I helped him look for small strategic shifts he could make that could create quick improvements, focusing on a few targeted areas. One of the first changes he made was to develop some bundled service packages. When he began offering these to potential customers, he noticed people accepted his pricing more quickly. While he wasn't tracking conversion rates yet, his closing rate improved right away.

He also started simple upsells. During his first week of trying it, he averaged around $300 in added services per customer and closed five of those sales in just a few days.

These techniques showed him that growth didn't have to mean working more hours. It could come from working smarter in the business he had already built.

A Question Worth Asking Yourself

What is one thing you can do or one change you can make this week, in each of these areas, to start increasing your profits?

_____

_____

_____

_____

_____

_____

Profit Growth Calculator™

Profit isn't a number you control directly; it's the result of many smaller actions you take every day. The _Profit Growth Calculator_™ helps you see how small improvements in leads, conversion rates, revenue per customer, and more can add up to big changes in your bottom line. You can download it at www.RootsandRiversBook.com/FreeTools and pinpoint specific actions you can take to grow your profits.

PRINCIPLE
THREE

Assemble and
Align Your Team

*How You Train and Guide the
People That Will Support You*

I've mentioned the owner of a canoe livery near Cincinnati who gave me my first entrepreneurial taste of the canoe business. Jim Thaxton has been in the canoe business since the 1970s. He's a true enthusiast. Not only does he (and now his family) run this water-sports business, but in his spare time he manages a competitive dragon boat racing team.

Based on ancient Chinese folk traditions dating back over two thousand years, dragon boating enthusiasts consider it to be the ultimate team-building experience. Picture a long, narrow, canoe-shaped boat, decorated with a dragon's head and tail, filled with typically twenty paddlers, sitting two by two, their oars slicing into the water in perfect rhythm. At the front of the boat is a drummer beating a steady pace that the team must follow. At the back stands the steersperson, guiding the boat with a large oar to keep it on course and calling out instructions to the team. When everything clicks, the boat almost seems to glide above the water.

What makes it so compelling is the team aspect. The strongest paddler in the boat can't make it move alone. And even the hardest-working team will lose momentum if they're not in sync. Success comes from everyone knowing their role, listening to the beat of the drum, and trusting that each stroke contributes to the whole. From the shore, you can see the intensity on every paddler's face, their muscles straining, but all of them moving together as one. It's a vivid picture of how individual effort and team alignment create something far greater than the sum of the parts.

This is a strong analogy for successfully building and leading a business team. To make real progress, you have to start with a clear understanding of your own strengths and weaknesses. In dragon boating, some paddlers are better suited for the front seats, setting the rhythm. Others thrive in the middle, where raw power drives the boat. Still others have the stamina for the back, keeping balance and endurance through the race. The same is true in business. You have to know where you're strongest, and where you need others to fill the gaps.

If the paddlers aren't aligned with the same rhythm, all you get is a lot of splash and wasted energy. In your business, this means taking the time to align everyone with the same goals and vision. If even a few people are pulling in a different direction, progress stalls, even if they are the most talented members of your team. When everyone rows to the same beat, momentum builds and the team moves faster than you imagined possible.

Finally, you can't just put anyone with an oar into the boat and hope for the best. The best dragon boat teams choose their paddlers carefully. They look for people who can learn, who will commit, and who will stay in rhythm with the rest of the crew. That's exactly what you have to do when you hire. Skills and talent matter, but if someone refuses to row with the team, they'll slow everyone down. The right people in the right seats, pulling together toward the same destination, make all the difference.

Like a dragon boat sweeping through the water, no business leader succeeds alone. Strengths must be balanced, goals must be aligned, and people must be chosen with care. When those elements come together, the boat moves. When they don't, you're left thrashing in the water, going nowhere real fast.

CHAPTER 10

Remodeling the Homeplace

When we moved to our homeplace, I felt like I was finally home. We'd lived in a one-street subdivision in a neighboring county for twenty years, but it never made me feel at home in the way my Place did.

The house itself needed serious updating, and we spent a couple years doing that, mostly ourselves. Besides the construction skills I learned, I got a real sense of accomplishment in doing this. I felt like I was making this place livable for the next generation, choosing remodeling decisions we felt were good for our kids, if any of them wanted to live there. (More detail on this later.)

I got to buy tools! The trips to Home Depot made me feel like a kid in a toy store. I spent hours agonizing over which miter saw to purchase, and when I finally decided, I brought it home, so proud of it. (Francie didn't seem quite as excited about it as I was.) I also spent several hours looking through woodworking magazines, trying to determine which jigs I needed to build to help me out. Actually, the mindset was more, "This is cool, how could I use this?" and I would build it, proudly bringing Francie out to the garage to show her my new masterpiece. Generally, she humored me, telling me it was nice and would really be helpful.

Over the years, I learned a lot of construction skills from my dad. He'd remodeled his home to make a sewing room for my mom, and he'd built a two-story shop, from scratch, which served as a sales floor for my mom's craft business. He had something of a mindset of doing everything himself, of being self-sufficient. If he didn't know how to do something, he'd learn. He'd buy some how-to books or ask someone who knew how to do it to show him. I think I inherited this trait from him.

He had an old beat-up Ford Ranger that had no muffler, so when I drove in to work in the evenings and on weekends, it wouldn't be but just a few minutes before I'd hear that old truck start up, and he'd drive down, asking what we were going to do today. We had a good time together. We'd talk about the work we were doing, and we'd discuss how to solve a problem that we'd run into. We had some intense discussions about what we were going to do about getting new electric lines through the existing plaster walls. We'd laugh at each other about how scroungy and dirty each of us seemed to get most days. We fussed about Uncle Eddie, because he'd painted over some old wallpaper, and complained about how hard it made it to remove.

We also spent a lot of time planning, and even though I was about fifty, it seemed it was the first time we'd had these conversations as equals, rather than as the all-knowing father instructing the son who was still learning. Granted, we still had those conversations too, because he had so much practical construction experience. We also had a few arguments—he thought I was being frivolous and wasting my time and effort by putting speaker wires into every room. Looking back, I can see his point. Music wasn't particularly important to him, not near like what it was for me. But since it was my house, I did win that argument!

This process gave me a new appreciation for the craftsmanship of construction tradesmen. As an example: The plaster walls throughout the whole house were pretty rough. I used some drywall mud to smooth it out, and it took me days and days to do that. I finally found someone who put on the third and final coat of drywall mud throughout the whole house. It cost me $300 and only took him a day to do it. It would have taken me three weeks. I should have had a professional do all of it!

All in all, I couldn't have done this without my dad. He had the skills. I had the desire, but not the deep abilities it took to do the extensive remodeling I wanted to do. By leveraging his knowledge, not only did I learn new skills, but I felt closer to him than ever before. We had a good time doing this together.

$$\Leftrightarrow$$

This story of remodeling my homeplace is a good analogy of what happens to nearly every new business owner. They've got all kinds of ideas running around in their head about what they could do and what they want this business to look like.

There's plenty of other business owners out there that have the same story. They start out not having the knowledge, and they don't have the money to hire someone to get it done, so they struggle trying to do it all themselves, sometimes for years.

I lucked out. I thought I could do all these things, and I knew my dad could help, but after I got into it, I realized I didn't have near the skill set I thought I had. But Dad was there to teach me, and it worked out all right.

Because of this experience, I learned the importance of tapping into the expertise of others. It's important to know your strengths, but it might be more important to objectively identify your weaknesses. Over time, I've learned (sometimes the hard way) that paying an IT person has saved me all kinds of headaches in dealing with computer and internet issues. A virtual assistant has been invaluable for me in taking care of things I could do but that are not the best use of my time and energy.

I've also learned that drawing on the abilities of other coaches over time has helped me learn some important skills to move my own business forward. I had coaches to help me learn business planning and lead generation skills. Others helped me make more effective presentations and become a more effective coach myself.

As I write this story, I have multiple coaches helping me grow. A coach from the UK is helping me ramp up my marketing efforts. A local leadership coach is holding me accountable in setting my most important priorities for self-management. Even now, writing this book, a coach is helping me refine my ideas and clarify my thoughts.

The Principle in Practice

The first step in ensuring you have the capability of moving forward with your business is understanding what you do well and determining what skills you may be lacking. This idea of a self-assessment seems straightforward enough, but it can be hard to do it accurately—and honestly.

A business skills assessment is important and relatively simple. Look over the various broad areas of a business plan. Which of these areas requires technical expertise you either have or don't have? To give yourself an indication as to where you need help, think through the challenges you're currently facing in your business.

It also helps to get a sense of your innate strengths. Do this by asking yourself, "What activities do I get the most satisfaction from, in what areas do I catch on quickly, and where do I naturally excel?"

Arguably, the most challenging part of this assessment is identifying what you don't know or don't do well. In Donald Clifton and Paula Nelson's book *Soar with Your Strengths*, the authors call out clues that can indicate a weakness, including a "have to" rather than a "want to" attitude toward a particular activity (and the lengths you would go to avoid doing it), not catching on very quickly, and not learning from experience.

Together, this assessment of business skills, and the identification of personal aptitudes, can help you determine how best to manage the areas of your business where you need the most help.

A Question Worth Asking Yourself

What are the biggest challenges you're facing in your business right now? What might that tell you about the biggest deficits in ability that you're facing?

_____

_____

_____

Strengths & Support Inventory™

It's tough to see both your strengths and weaknesses clearly when you're busy running a business. The _Strengths & Support Inventory_™ can help you honestly assess what you do well and where you might need help, so you can focus your energy and resources where they matter most.

Visit www.RootsandRiversBook.com/FreeTools to download this practical worksheet. It's the first step to building a stronger business by working from your strengths, as well as knowing where to get help when you need it.

As I mentioned, I currently have multiple coaches helping me grow in areas where I need help. Maybe you could use some help as well. If so, book a call with me at www.25withkim.com, and let's talk about how a business coach might help you up your game.

CHAPTER 11

Father/Son Conflict

I was a kid growing up on a farm, so it was expected that I would help with farmwork. It almost always included summertimes and weekends, and it sometimes included early mornings and holidays. As a teenager, I wanted to do other things, like play basketball, read, or sleep in. Understandably, Dad didn't have much patience with that.

As a young adult, the work ethic he'd tried to instill in me finally paid off, and I took the initiative of raising Dad's tobacco crop as a tenant. I did this part-time, driving over from the next county after my full-time job was over for the day.

As a tenant farmer, I provided the labor, and in our case, the landowner provided both the land and the equipment.

Now, a common trait among farmers is that they can fix almost anything. This is largely due to necessity, as most small farmers have older equipment. The tradeoff of not paying for expensive new equipment is that the old equipment always breaks down.

My dad had that ability to fix anything. I didn't. I'd come home to work in the crop in the late afternoon, and invariably, a piece of equipment I needed would be broken down. It wouldn't start, or the tire was flat, and I would have to wait for him to stop what he was doing and fix it. I'd get annoyed at having to wait on him, and he'd get annoyed at me for being annoyed with him. It was a working relationship underlaid with tension.

I've already mentioned the canoe livery. It was moderately successful for me, and it turned into a good side business for Dad's campground for a number of years. But I was again doing this on Dad's property and using his resources. Over time, these tensions mounted again. He (rightly) felt I was depending too much on him and, to some degree, taking advantage of him being there all the time.

All this took place when I was in my mid-to-late twenties. It wasn't until I was about fifty that I moved back to my homeplace, and as I related in the last chapter, the dynamic between Dad and me shifted during our time spent remodeling.

I think he was as excited about us moving as I was. This house was his homeplace as well; he'd lived there since he was six years old. He lived on the same property and had a sentimental attachment to the place probably even more than I did, and now his son was moving back home. We had a good time, working together as we did.

Having in the back of my mind that I would eventually take over his campground, I would try to help him with some things. I learned the electrical and plumbing systems, and I did some competition and pricing research, among other specifics.

When I took over the management of the business the weekend he went into the hospital, the changes I made greatly increased the profitability of that business. These changes also made some of the campers mad. They'd gotten used to the looser management of the past few years and didn't really want to change. When Dad got better and was ultimately able to come home, he got an earful of the complaints.

I did what I had felt needed to be done, but Dad didn't see it that way. He was upset with me, and the near-constant criticism from him about my actions, my judgement, and my motives was getting on my nerves. I was doing this to honor my parents' legacy, but Dad saw it as me undoing what he was trying to accomplish. His mission with the business had shifted to helping people who were down on their luck—people who were homeless or who were trying to recover from addictions or some other misfortune. I was looking to run this as a business that needed to show a profit, and that couldn't include people who couldn't pay.

While he had given me permission to take over the campground, he decided to rescind that permission, even to the point of setting up his estate so Kevin and I would have no part of the business after he was gone.

When Francie and I moved to our Place, one of my justifications for doing so was to take care of my aging parents (when the time came) and to help dad with his campground when he needed me. I had served that role, but now, Dad had given that responsibility to someone else.

For a few years, we struggled with the conflicting need to be there for my dad and our desire to be closer to our grandkids, who lived in another state. With dad's decision, he removed that struggle. We no longer had to take care of my dad or his business, and we decided it was time to move, but I'll tell that story later in this book.

⬖

Multiple generations of family that have been able to resolve inevitable differences in management styles and values are to be looked up to, in my opinion. I have a lot of respect for them.

As a young adult, even before I had any business skills to speak of, I had natural tendencies that didn't mesh well with my dad. A lack of order and organization didn't seem to bother him, but it was quite frustrating to me. Both the tobacco crop and the canoe business were my priorities, not his. He quit raising a crop because he was tired of it, but he agreed to help me because I wanted to, and he had enough to do without me adding my canoe idea to his list of responsibilities.

Tendencies are important, but deeper than that is the reason why the business exists, its purpose. The two of us were at odds on this, and unfortunately, we never talked about it. Dad's farm and campground investment was paid for, his standard of living was relatively modest, and he was interested in providing a place for people to live who couldn't afford anyplace else. When I took over, I saw that the campground could not support a scenario of either parent having to pay for long-term nursing care. I also had the mindset of operating at a higher level of profit than he did. I wanted a successful business. He wanted a place that supported the homeless. Our ideas on why this business existed were not aligned, and because of this, we were not destined to work well together.

The Principle in Practice

If two or more people are to succeed as partners, they need to have a purpose for being that aligns with each other.

A strong purpose helps you stay grounded when things get tough, and it provides some anchoring power when you make choices. Stephen Covey, in *The 7 Habits of Highly Effective People*, says, in all simplicity, "The main thing is to keep the main thing the main thing." When a potential decision or a direction doesn't align with your purpose, it's a lot easier to say no.

A statement of purpose is sometimes mistaken for a mission statement. A mission says *what* you do. Your purpose outlines *why* you do it—your True North. It's not written in marketing language. It outlines your reason for showing up every day, even when no one's looking.

When your work serves something bigger than yourself, it helps you better endure the long hours, setbacks, and stresses that naturally come with running a business. When you effectively share this with your team, it brings them together and gets them working toward something beyond just a paycheck, which can be a beautiful thing.

People are drawn to a business that stands for something. Simon Sinek underscores the business value of articulating and living out a strong, public-facing purpose in his book *Start with Why*. He says, "People don't buy what you do; they buy why you do it."

When your purpose and your partner's purpose don't match, you'll be pulling in different directions, and eventually, something's going to give: either the business or the relationship. This is what my dad and I experienced during our time managing the campground.

Defining your True North takes reflection. Ask yourself why you started this business in the first place. What problem were you trying to solve and who were you trying to help?

If you came upon a good inheritance or won the lottery, would you still do this work? Why? What makes all the stress and the hard work feel worth it? If someone offered to buy you out with a price that was more than fair, but they were planning to dismantle the business and erase all it stood for, what would be your reaction, and why?

When you answer these kinds of questions, you've identified the heartbeat of why you do what you do. Now, simplify it. Cut it down to one or two sentences, using plain emotional language. Make it real and make it personal. Test it: Does it give you a lump in your throat when you read it out loud?

This statement ultimately shapes your reputation; it becomes what you're known for. You've carefully crafted it to be concise and inspirational. Now, communicate it continuously with everyone you work with, in staff newsletters, written materials, emails, staff meetings, and trainings.

Dave Lavinsky, in *Start at the End*, states, "It takes courage to share your vision. It forces you to take a stand." So take that stand. Create a company culture based on this True North vision. Integrate it throughout your business, using it as an evaluation for any decision that is made, whether that's hiring, or goal setting, or marketing, or operational decisions.

How Others Have Put This to Work

One of the first businesses I worked with was a partnership of three close friends, each with very different strengths. Their senior move company had reached a point where roles were unclear, and they were unsure about the commitments each person needed to make, both to the business and to one another. They knew they needed a way to work through it.

Through a guided planning process, they began to define their individual roles based on their own skill sets. It gave them the structure and language to hold each other accountable without damaging their friendship. In fact, they later told me that learning to challenge each other professionally helped them grow even closer personally.

They also began to see something bigger: If the business was going to grow, they would need to step out of the daily hands-on work and focus more intentionally on leadership. That shift gave them the freedom to work on the business instead of being the ones who were actually moving people.

That alignment rippled outward. One of the partners shared how rewarding it was to see their team take ownership and feel proud of a job well done. By stepping back, they were able to empower their employees to assume more of a leadership role themselves.

A Question Worth Asking Yourself

Why are you in the business you're in, beyond the obvious profit-motive?

_____

_____

_____

_____

_____

_____

True North Compass™

The questions I asked above aren't easy. If this idea of writing your own _True North Compass_™ feels overwhelming, I've put together a simple worksheet to help you get started.

Visit www.RootsandRiversBook.com/FreeTools to download a few thoughtful questions to help you look back, look ahead, sort through what really matters, and start putting words around those thoughts.

CHAPTER 12

Depending on Others

Farming is a lifestyle. But it is one intensive lifestyle. Day in and day out, you're at the mercy of the weather. Payday doesn't come often—in the case of crops, maybe once a year. Because of that, many farmers have a full-time job off the farm to help pay the monthly bills.

Dad was no different. As I was growing up, at times, he worked for the state, he drove a school bus, and he worked for a non-profit. In order to make sure farmwork got done in a timely manner, he hired a tenant who lived on the farm.

Mr. and Mrs. Baker lived in a trailer across from our house, and Mr. Baker raised the tobacco crop and helped Dad with the cattle. I was only a kid when he lived there, but even so, I could tell Mr. Baker showed a lot of responsibility for the crops, and he cared for the land, treating it as if it was his own property.

Later, in the late 1960s, when I was a young teenager, Dad raised tomatoes for a canning factory nearby. Harvesting tomatoes by hand was a hot, hard, back-breaking job, and there's a short window of time when it needs to be done. (Half a century later, I can still smell the stench of tomatoes that were laying on the ground and starting to rot.)

Dad hired several older teenagers and young adults to help him with this. He treated them well, and they in turn worked hard, but they also had a lot of fun doing it. I remember Dad and these boys getting into a few tomato fights in the field. (Picture a snowball fight, but in the summer and using ripe tomatoes.) I suppose that cut the efficiency of the harvest slightly, but it was what helped make for a good working environment, and it's the memory I think of after all these years.

When Dad started the campground, he hired some of the resident campers to help out with odd jobs around the place, particularly cutting grass, weedeating, working in the camp office, and keeping the showerhouse clean. They did a good job, in large part because they cared for the place, which was because Dad ran it in such a way that it attracted people who were interested in being part of a community.

As he aged, and as Mom's Parkinson's progressed to the point she couldn't take care of herself, Dad hired some female campers to help with her care. In this case, he wasn't as successful. Not all of her caregivers had Mom's best interests at heart. They wouldn't show up at times, putting Dad in a bind, because he couldn't leave her to go out and work. They tended to help themselves to the cash box occasionally, and when they learned my dad was rather tender-hearted, they'd often come up with a sob-story and convince him to lend them money, which, of course, they never paid back.

After I took over, one of these so-called caregivers was still around, and while it took longer than it should have (mostly because I wasn't aggressive enough), I finally got her out of the house and off the property.

At this point, Mom was nearing the end of her life, and she needed permanent care. I hired a resident nurse, who specialized in end-of-life home care, and she stayed with Mom constantly for six days a week. (Kevin and I stayed with her on the nurse's day off.) I felt very fortunate to have found this lady, whose name was Alida. She was very conscientious in what she did, caring for Mom and caring for the house like she was family.

Taking over the campground came about suddenly, and it took me a few weeks to adjust to the new job. On a professional basis, I had started this fledgling business coaching firm, and my head was filled with ideas on how to make it grow, which I quickly had to put on hold. While I had been helping Dad with some big picture stuff, I had not been particularly involved in the day-to-day operations, so I had a steep learning curve there, and it required a lot of my attention.

It was tough emotionally, as well. My dad was critically sick, and I was driving to the hospital nearly every day to spend time with him, waiting to see doctors who sometimes seemed to give conflicting advice. Mom also continued to decline and needed constant care, and I worried about doing the right thing for her.

My first month managing the campground, there was a drowning and a major fish-kill on the river, all in one week, and we had two campers getting into constant fights that the sheriff had to get involved in.

Luckily, one of Mom's caregivers, Michelle, was highly professional, and Dad had started depending on her to take reservations, collect money, and see that his customers were cared for. She did this well.

Within that first month, I asked her to take the job as campground manager, and she agreed. This turned out to be a good move. She genuinely cared for the place and loved Mom and Dad, and she wanted to do her part to build it up as a legacy for them.

As we were both learning how to do this, she readily agreed to help me develop some needed systems. She also took the initiative to have tough conversations with campers who had been taking advantage of Dad's preoccupation with caring for Mom, and, consequently, his lack of management. After I left the campground, she stayed on for several more years and was a vital asset to the whole operation.

That summer, fall, and winter of running the campground also gave me the opportunity to work closely with Kevin. My brother lived about two hours away, but he came in every weekend and stayed numerous times through the week to help get things done. His mechanical and tractor skills were much better than mine, and he respected my business management skills. We had a great year together. During the day, we spent our time working, and in the evenings, we shared a glass of bourbon, reflecting on the day's efforts and planning for the next day and the next year. That time with him was a real blessing.

⬖

Hiring people you already know is easy. It's great when it works out, but it becomes a real challenge when, for one reason or another, it doesn't work out.

Dad, for a long time, felt like his Christian duty was to help people who were down on their luck. He helped numerous people get back on their feet, and they've been very grateful to him, but sometimes this backfired and people took advantage of him, including a few people he had employed.

Seeing those interactions helped me realize it is vitally important that job responsibilities and expectations be formally outlined before any hire, especially if that new hire is someone I already know or someone who was recommended by a friend.

Over the years, my natural tendency has been "I know them and they'll be okay" or "They come highly recommended so I don't need to go through all this paperwork." What I've finally learned is, this formality can protect me in case my initial opinion of the person turns out to be inaccurate.

It's good for the employee as well. Anyone starting a new job needs to know what's expected of them, and what constitutes good work. If a job description is formalized, there is no question as to what is expected.

People you work with every day become more than employees. When you have a good working relationship that is based on formal expectations and responsibilities, you come to depend on them. You get to know them better. You come to appreciate their skills, their abilities, and their insights. They're providing you a way to help grow your business, but maybe more importantly, they're enriching your life, and you're doing the same for them.

With these kinds of benefits in mind, it's easy to see that you and the employee both deserve to have this kind of structure in place.

The Principle in Practice

In Mel Kleiman's well-regarded book *Hire Tough, Manage Easy*, he quotes a very successful serial entrepreneur: "I only have one job, and that's to hire the right people. If I do that well, I don't have to do anything else!"

The first step in a recruiting process is to know exactly what kind of person you want. This goes beyond a listing of required responsibilities and skills. It also includes the personal dispositions and temperament a person must possess to meet the demands of the job and be successful at it.

An important principle in hiring is that you treat it the same way you would for marketing, with the goal of generating a *lot* of leads on high quality employees by using a *lot* of recruitment tactics.

To generate those leads, you need an ad that describes the opportunity with words that *really* attract potential employees. "Help wanted" just doesn't cut it. You need to entice people to desire this job. Then you need to get that job ad posted in many different places, where good potential employees would be.

Once you have a good employee, you want to keep them. Patrick Lencioni, in his insightful book *The Truth About Employee Engagement*, suggests three ways to do that:

1. Show you care. Get to know them personally; what they like in terms of work, what they enjoy outside work, details about their family and friends. This takes genuine curiosity, deep listening, and some one-on-one time. Understand them, not just because of what they do for you, but because they

are unique individuals with hopes and dreams, doubts and imperfections, and a beautiful, complex soul.

2. Provide purpose. People need meaning. Show them how their work contributes to the bigger purpose beyond profit. Be thoughtful and specific, offering more than just a quick "great job."

3. Measure progress. People need to see that they are moving forward. Help them find ways to measure their own performance and hold themselves accountable, with some form of reward when they meet those goals.

I want to add a fourth way: You have to be clear. If people don't know where they stand, they can't grow. Offer direct, honest feedback, set clear expectations, and follow through. When you're consistently clear, people feel safe, because they trust you to tell them the truth.

Some employees may not buy into this. That's okay. If you're changing the culture of your workplace and they don't want to change, it's better to part ways and move on.

How Others Have Put This to Work

A shop-based business owner had one employee with such a bad attitude, it was poisoning the whole atmosphere of the workplace. This entrepreneur had a good business, but he was on the verge of selling the business just to escape the stress. He was ready to give up.

With my help, he tried engaging his whole staff in a few key areas mentioned above. Over time, the atmosphere began to shift. He said, "For the first time in a long time, I've seen smiles on EACH of the team members' faces this week. Morale is up. It's actually fun to come into work again!"

Not only did that change improve the workplace, it also gave him a renewed energy for the business itself. What once felt frustrating began to feel hopeful again, and he's still running the business. That renewed employee engagement has also allowed him to get away from the shop more often, with the assurance that these employees will keep things running smoothly while he's gone.

A Question Worth Asking Yourself

How well do your employees enjoy coming into work every day? What could you do to make it better?

_____

_____

_____

_____

_____

_____

Engagement Activation Guide™

Team morale doesn't improve by chance. If your workplace feels heavy or stuck, it's time to take action. I created the _Engagement Activation Guide_™ to help you think through what makes employees feel valued, connected, and energized. Visit www.RootsandRiversBook.com/FreeTools to download this practical tool and start building a stronger, more committed team, one simple action at a time.

PRINCIPLE FOUR
Cultivate Contentment

*Your Efforts in Making Time for
Self, Satisfaction, and Purpose*

I imagine you're familiar with Charles Dickens' classic story *A Christmas Carol*. Ebenezer Scrooge was a "squeezing, wrenching, grasping, scraping, clutching, covetous old sinner" who didn't believe in charity and didn't see the error of his ways until the Christmas Eve visits of three ghosts showed Scrooge what his acquaintances truly thought of him.

Most of us know people that remind us of Mr. Scrooge. When I led a program on writing mission statements some twenty years ago, one of the businessman participants in this seminar stood up, bluntly and arrogantly stating that his mission statement was to make as much money as possible in as little time as possible, and that I was wasting his time talking about all this touchy-feely stuff.

I was just getting started teaching business principles and didn't yet have much experience in dealing with someone who was contemptuous of what I said. His statement took me aback; I don't recall what I said to get out of this uncomfortable moment, but I do remember having Scrooge come to mind and actually feeling sorry for the guy. Later, I heard others talking disdainfully, over drinks, about this guy's statement too. I don't know what they thought of him before, but they sure didn't have much respect for him that evening!

The whole point of having a business is to provide a better life for yourself. That life includes profit, for sure, but it also includes what you can do with that profit to make your small part of the world a better place. As I pointed out a few chapters ago, my dad's motivation was nonprofit-oriented. He wanted to help the homeless, and that became his mission later in life.

Writing this book, I think of my own journey: the values that are important to me and the constant struggle to truly live them out, the respect I'd like others to have for me, and the respect I'd like to have for myself. I consider myself a giving person, but I also recognize there has to be a line between what I give away and what I get paid for providing. Where should that line be? Do I gain respect for giving away my service, or do I lose respect as a credible businessperson by giving away too much of what I sell?

I feel comfortable stating I'm a really good coach. Part of the way I work with prospective clients is by actually coaching them through some business-related or personal challenges they have. Instead of telling them what I do, I show them what I do, so they can get a real sense of what it'd be like to work with me. Some of my own coaches over time have cautioned me about that, with the idea that, if you fix their problem before they invest in you, they have no more need for you, and you just lost a sale.

I've struggled with that. My values are important, but they aren't worth much if I don't live them. At the same time, I need to be satisfied with what I'm doing. I need to have the contentment that comes from providing a service I'm good at providing, but I also need to generate enough revenue to make it worth my while financially.

There's a quote attributed to Ralph Waldo Emerson that I absolutely believe: "The mind, once stretched by a new idea, never returns to its original dimensions." Bob Burg and John David Mann's *The Go-Giver* recently stretched my mind, helping me find a solution to the conflict between my values and business, giving me permission to adjust my written Core Values to reflect this generosity of service. Their book offered me a way forward in my desire to gain respect without compromising what I stood for.

For many small business owners, their business is more than just a business; it's part of their lives. They've come up with the idea for it, and they have an emotional attachment to it. Even if they purchased it from someone else, they've put their own creative bent into it.

This is particularly acute when the business is also the owner's home or property (businesses like a farm, a campground, an inn, or a bed and breakfast). This also applies to legacy businesses (ones that have been in the family for generations).

The business lessons in the other sections of this book deal with logical, analytical parts of operating a business—the What and the How. This section focuses on the emotion behind the logic, outlining the Why. It may arguably be the most important part of the book.

CHAPTER 13

Decision to Move to Virginia

My daughter was the fifth generation of my family that lived in our home, but she was also destined to be the last generation that lived there. As our kids grew up and started their own adult lives, they followed their own dreams. Those dreams did not include a family homeplace on the river.

Our oldest daughter had started a family in northern Virginia, our son also lived in that area at the time, and our youngest daughter had started her life as a city girl in Manhattan. We could dream, but in reality, they weren't coming home again. On average, about every two months, Francie and I would hop in the car and make the nine-to-ten-hour trip to northern Virginia to get to know our grandkids. When we arrived on our visits, we'd come in the door for the first time, and our grandkids would run to us and give us a big bear hug, and they'd immediately start telling us what they were doing. Pretty quickly, they'd "convince" me to get down on my hands and knees and give them a horsey ride, holding on as I pretended to try to buck them off, and begging to keep going when the old horsey finally gave out and had to collapse on the floor.

Grandparenting was every bit what it was cracked up to be! Sitting in the rocker holding them, and them telling us all about their day. Reading to them. Helping them learn to ride bikes. Tossing a football. Helping them learn how to use some basic tools to put together their own dresser. Taking them to the playground. Taking them fishing. Taking them to go get ice cream with sprinkles on it. Working puzzles. Having serious discussions about cars, dinosaurs, Godzilla, and Barbies.

Living two states away, we were missing out, and we gradually came to the realization that we would need to make a major life change we hadn't anticipated. While Place was important, Family was more important. And with the kids living as far from us as they did, with little chance of them ever coming back, we were going to have to give up the Place to be able to have that closer connection to Family.

For several years, as Francie and I traveled back and forth to Virginia, we began using each trip as something of a "scouting" trip, in that we'd visit some mid-sized towns with the mindset of "how might we like living here."

We liked my hometown of Frankfort. When we started looking for places where we might like to live that were close to family, Frankfort became our model. We wanted to find someplace that had a similar ambiance, in which the downtown had character. It was also important to find a place that had a river close by and a vibrant Catholic faith community.

We also looked for places with history to them. In our travels, we toured Civil War sites, visiting nearly all the National Park Service battlefields in Maryland and Virginia. In fact, a battlefield is how we got our first taste of the town to which we ultimately moved.

These "scouting trips" kept the possibilities of a future move in our minds, but that future didn't have any time frame attached to it. Once Dad removed my responsibilities toward him, we decided that the time had come to make the choice we'd been toying with.

The emotional ties to my Place were difficult to break. I had spent three years remodeling this house. I was proud of my craftsmanship, and it felt like it was a part of me. I'd done it for Francie and me, but I'd also done it for future generations, hoping against hope that one day my kids and grandkids might want to come back.

We had the family legacy of five generations in one house, and I was the one breaking that legacy. My kids wouldn't have this place as an anchor for themselves, and I felt like I was abandoning my memories and family traditions. I know life moves on and changes always have to be made, but in a sense, I was giving up my birthright—and one of the most beautiful spots on earth.

No longer would I sit outside with my wife on a warm spring day, enjoying the river and the landscaping I'd worked hard on, listening to Jimmy Buffett on the outside speakers. No longer would I sit in my hammock in the shade on weekends, reading a western and watching people enjoy water skiing and tubing on the river—my river. No longer would we drive into Frankfort on a Friday night, enjoying an outdoor summer concert on the Old Capital lawn, visiting my friends and colleagues, and enjoying the feel of my vibrant downtown community.

Those were the negative emotions of leaving our Place, but logic helped us deal with it. We no longer had any obligation to stay to help Dad out with the campground or with his health and end-of-life decisions. I was getting old enough that keeping up with the extensive landscaping would become harder to manage. Luckily, we hadn't had flood waters in the house while we lived there, but we recognized we were living on borrowed time with that (three years, as it turned out; flood waters got three feet into the house in April 2025).

The move to Virginia also gave us new opportunities. Our youngest daughter lived in New York City, and we could easily take the train to visit her and her husband, and experience life there with insiders, not as tourists. Francie and I also satisfied some bucket-list items like going to concerts at several iconic jazz clubs.

All of a sudden, I now had a whole new state to get to know. Coastal areas, mountain foothills, urban landscapes, and new quaint villages within a couple hours of where we lived. Virginia does wineries and breweries well, and there were a host of rivers to delve into: the Rappahannock, the Potomac, the Shenandoah, the James, and the Jackson, as well as the Chesapeake Bay.

And we know our grandkids far better than we would have if we'd stayed in Kentucky. We've been to grandparent's day at school, attended our oldest grandson's football game, and taken our middle grandson fishing on the spur of the moment. We've also been there for our daughter when she needed us during last minute emergencies.

With the move, we left Dad physically, but not emotionally. The rather strained relationship gnawed at me. I'd call occasionally, and when we went back to Kentucky, I'd stop by and see him, but the conversation was always superficial. I sensed he was lonely, and while I felt bad for him, those feelings were tempered by the idea that he'd done this to himself, which in turn was tempered by my own guilt that I should have handled it differently.

Despite our differences, I wanted to be there with Dad when his time on earth came to an end, but I realized that with us now a day's travel away, this was going to be some feat of accomplishment. Francie and I had both been at my mother's bedside at home when she took her last breath, but we lived on the same property and I was there every day. Under our new circumstances, this would be entirely in God's hands. My prayer eventually became, "Lord, if it be your will, let me be there with him when he passes, but if that's not your will, help me to be okay with that."

One Friday afternoon in the late summer of 2025 (about the time I was putting the finishing touches on this book,) we got a call from a friend of his at the campground. They'd taken him to the emergency room, and it seemed serious. It just so happened that my kids were all in town visiting, and they helped me objectively decide the best thing I needed to do.

Early Saturday morning, Francie and I left the house on the fastest drive to Kentucky I think we've ever made. On the way, I got a call from a doctor who explained his health challenges, and he said it would be a miracle if he recovered. He didn't think he would survive in time for us to get there.

I believe in miracles, but I don't particularly feel comfortable praying for a miracle for a person in a 93-year-old body that's worn out.

But a miracle did happen. It came in the form of modern medicine and some caring hospital staff who purposefully kept him alive until we got there. Francie and I were able to spend about an hour with him before he passed.

It appears it was God's will that I be there with him in the end after all, to help provide some closure.

$$\Leftrightarrow$$

As you can probably tell, this move to a new state caused a lot of emotional turmoil. It still does, to some extent. I'm a Kentuckian. I miss my home state. I miss my afternoons sitting outside with Francie, watching my river go by. I miss the home we spent so much time and care in making ours and honoring our heritage. I miss my late evenings sitting outside by the firepit, listening to some Sinatra on the outdoor speakers, watching the lightning bugs and gazing up at the Milky Way. I miss my Place.

On the other hand, I enjoy my new exploring opportunities. I enjoy kayaking on my new river. I enjoy being the bourbon enthusiast from Kentucky. I enjoy becoming a part of my new hometown. I enjoy taking the train up north to visit my daughter in the city. I enjoy being able, at the drop of a hat, to see our grandkids, and to be a vital part of their life in a way that would not have been possible before our move.

It boils down to a major conflict in values. A conflict between Place and Family. A conflict between right vs. right, between two ideals that deeply matter.

Both Place and Family are part of my identity. I had to sacrifice one to be true to the other. It was a hard decision, but I suppose it shows the complexity of being human and making the right choices.

There's still internal tension. A lingering guilt that I'm so far away from my brother and good friends. A longing for the peace and quiet and beauty of our Place. But ultimately, this decision has helped me learn that life moves on. It might even be preparing me for another move, when I'm older and need help taking care of myself. And I'd like to think it's built character and helped me become a better person.

The Principle in Practice

Leadership is full of trade-offs. Sometimes, hard decisions have to be made between conflicting values. This requires some careful discernment.

It also requires you to identify those values before those decisions come up. If you don't, that decision is going to be based not on your purpose, but on external pressures: what others expect, what seems easiest at the moment, what seems safe. A decision not based on that internal grounding may not hold up over time.

We all yearn to contribute to something bigger than ourselves. A business that has carefully determined what they stand for stands out. Values provide a business with principles they can apply, not just policies to enforce. When your values are clear, your decisions are clearer, even the tough ones.

In his influential books *Good to Great* and *Built to Last*, Jim Collins claims you don't set your core values, you discover them. Great companies refine the values that are already inherent in the culture and the people within.

To do this, make a list of your heroes and mentors, living or dead, who mean something to you. Write down the characteristics you admire in each of these people. Look for the commonalities and narrow them down to four core characteristics.

Think back to a time in your business when you felt most proud, not because of the result but because of how you did something. Describe what made it meaningful to you.

Why did you start your business? I'm not talking about the market opportunity or income potential; I'm talking about the change or the contribution you wanted to make.

These questions may be difficult for you to answer, and it might require several attempts to discover your values. Resist holding onto words you think you *should* select, and use those that are true to you.

Brene Brown, in her book *Dare to Lead*, suggests the right values will give you a "deep resonance of self-identification." She suggests asking yourself: Does this truly define me? Is this who I am at my best? Is this a filter that helps me make hard decisions?

For values to mean anything, they must sometimes cause discomfort. Ask yourself, *what are three slippery, tempting behaviors that are outside each of your listed values?* and describe an example of a time when you did not fully live according to that value.

A Question Worth Asking Yourself

What values drive your business's culture? When was the last time living your values forced you to make a decision that went against a pure profit motive?

_____

_____

_____

_____

_____

Core Values Finder™

Some of the hardest leadership decisions are value-based trade-offs. If you haven't done the work to name those values in advance, it's easy to default to what's easiest or what might be expected in a value-less environment. The _Core Values Finder_™ can help you think through what really matters to you, narrow it down to a few guiding principles, and build a solid foundation for future decisions. Visit www.RootsandRiversBook.com/FreeTools to download this worksheet to help you ensure your business decisions reflect what matters most, not just what's most convenient.

CHAPTER 14

Uncle Eddie and Okinawa

Easter Sunday, April 1, 1945, about half a million troops landed in Okinawa for one of the last battles of World War II. These troops included my Uncle Eddie, who was a replacement corpsman with a company of Maine Raiders. They experienced terrible things over the next eighty-three days, and those memories affected Uncle Eddie his whole life.

As I mentioned earlier in this book, Uncle Eddie was the only member of his company that came out unscathed, at least physically. In his later years, he'd come to terms with those memories, and he could talk about them. The stories he shared with me were incredible.

After Okinawa, he was with the first wave of soldiers that landed on the island of Japan. He was there with the occupational forces for several months, and sometime after Christmas of 1945, he returned home.

On the evening of July 4, 1946, some fishing camp customers were setting off fireworks, and the noise got to him, bringing back memories he'd been able to push aside. He went into his upstairs bedroom that evening and started writing. What he wrote was a day-by-day account of his experiences in that battle. He said it was so real and so vivid in his memory that he could write this chronological autobiography as if it had happened yesterday. He even remembered what he had to eat on various days. He put his memories on paper through late May of the battle, and then he quit. Looking back on it, he said he supposed that was his self-therapy, the way he processed the experience he lived through and came to terms with it. When he quit writing, he'd done what he'd needed to, and it was time to move on.

I remember a classmate of mine in elementary school had a jacket he wore every day. It had been sent to him by his older brother, who was serving in Vietnam. This jacket was very colorful, with a map of Vietnam on the back and a couple of dragons, and the statement, "When I die I'll go to Heaven, because I've spent my time in Hell." Reading through Uncle Eddie's story, he gives a raw account of the absolute hell he lived through for nearly three months. Statements like:

> "Early the next morning I was awakened by rain dripping in my face. A moment later, I realized I was lying in water about three inches deep."

> "I grabbed my medical kit and got over to them. One was lying on the ground with his brains about five feet away from his head."

> "I got up and ate a can of C-rations. It tasted awful."

"It was so dark that I wasn't sure just what condition he was in. I suppose I more or less felt his wounds rather than saw them. I remember feeling the warm, rather sticky blood all over his legs and head and on my hands."

"I heard the call for Corpsman again . . . I ran to his foxhole . . . he was trying to talk to me, but I couldn't understand what he was trying to say . . . I thought of the times we had gone swimming off Guadalcanal and the talks we had had together. I felt very sorry for him, but I was also aware of the fact that it didn't affect me at all—it was just too bad—that's all."

"We'd lost track of the date at that time, and I was wondering if I were 21 yet, or if I would live to be 21."

(While all of these are from Uncle Eddie's handwritten account, now housed at the Kentucky Historical Society, a few were published in Mark Littleton and Chuck Wright's book, *Doc*, an account of numerous stories from medics in several wars, published in 2005.)

One thing stuck with Uncle Eddie. He told me about it numerous times, and his day-by-day memoir highlighted it. The day they landed, they walked by this great big field of wild lilies—Easter lilies—a flower native to Okinawa. He commented on it to other members of his company.

Now think about this. A replacement in a company of Marine Raiders—the toughest of the tough. They'd seen a lot of action in the last year or so, and were pretty jaded with life. Uncle Eddie mentioned they teased him about that comment. He didn't say whether that teasing was good-natured or not, but I suspect it wasn't.

As the weeks went on, he earned their respect. Respect that carried on for a lifetime. Nearly sixty years later, at his funeral, one of the members of his company sent flowers to his funeral. Not just any flower. This guy sent lilies. The funeral was in November, and he went to the effort of finding a florist who could send lilies!

On a cold, overcast November day, in a plot shared by his parents on a high hill overlooking the State Capitol building and the Kentucky River as it meanders through Frankfort, Uncle Eddie was laid to rest with military honors. Two soldiers in full uniform, in slow, precise movements, folded the flag which lay on the coffin, then stood at attention while the local honor guard provided a 21-gun salute, and a bugler on the next hillside played Taps. The soldiers presented the flag to the family, thanking us for Uncle Eddie's service to the country, and I now have that flag, along with Uncle Eddie's dogtags, framed on my office wall.

◈

I still get a lump in my throat thinking about that funeral—about the solemn pageantry of the honor guard, the lonesome sound of that far-off bugler, and the personal honor exhibited by a fellow soldier who remembered Uncle Eddie's dedication to his craft and to his own band of brothers more than a half century earlier.

I think Uncle Eddie gained that respect by doing his job well, by putting others before himself. In his case, that meant putting his life in danger to rescue someone else. And in spite of his comment in his personal battle narrative of how watching a friend die didn't affect him that much, the rest of his actions in those three months showed he cared. The fact that he even mentioned it suggested a disappointment in his own lack of emotion, and may well reflect a soldier's mechanism to continue doing what they have to do in those horrific conditions.

I think of my dad's customers at his campground. Their respect for him showed up regularly in social media posts about the campground, and it happened because he cared about them personally far more than he cared about them as a customer. He celebrated with them. He'd bend over backwards to help them, and he'd charge less than he should've because he was concerned some of them couldn't afford a higher price. In past floods, he pulled out their RV's before he moved his own belongings to higher ground. He was selfless with them, and they recognized that.

All this makes me consider: How can I gain the respect of the people I work with, the people I serve? What must I do to gain the respect that would last a lifetime? Every Easter, when I see the collection of lilies that Uncle Eddie liked so well around the altar at church, I'm reminded: What are the actions I must take to garner that kind of respect from those people who are important to me?

The Principle in Practice

Obtaining lifelong respect from customers requires more than a great product or service. It's about embodying values that create trust and credibility. It's about creating a lasting emotional connection.

Actions to gain respect that lasts a lifetime are going to be different for every business, as well as every business owner, but there are several ways to achieve a respect that spans across all areas of your business.

First and foremost, you need to operate with an unwavering level of commitment to your values. Jon Huntsman Jr., in his book *Winners Never Cheat*, states that "There are no moral shortcuts in the game of business, or life. There are, basically, three kinds of people: the unsuccessful, the temporarily successful, and those who become and remain successful. The difference is character."

This level of integrity means keeping your promises, even when it's hard, and owning your mistakes when you fall short.

Make your business stand for something bigger than yourself. Define your purpose and lead others in your business with that purpose. Actively define what you must do every single day to live that purpose.

Give generously of your time, knowledge, and resources. Surprise people with values they don't expect and act with their interests in mind. Strive to be exceptional in what you do. Offer lasting solutions, grow in your competence, and be a trusted source of wisdom for your customers and all others who could benefit from it.

Stay humble. Share your story, including your mistakes, and show how you learned from them. Listen well. Make customers feel heard and valued, and let their feedback guide your improvements.

Be different and memorable. Innovate. Create experiences that will delight your customers at every single step. Make your business unforgettable. Build a reputation as the go-to expert in your field.

Create traditions and build a community. Make every interaction with your customer something more than just a transaction.

A Question Worth Asking Yourself

What do YOU need to do to gain the respect of the people you work with, the people you serve?

_____

_____

_____

_____

_____

_____

Values-in-Action Plan™

Respect that lasts comes from values that are lived out, not just talked about. Our _Values-in-Action Plan_™, available at <u>www.RootsandRiversBook.com/FreeTools</u>, is a practical worksheet to help you connect your stated values to your actual decisions, actions, and habits. This can give you a good start on making sure the way you lead, serve, and work aligns with what you truly believe.

CHAPTER 15

Hoosier Roots

There's a little town in Southern Indiana called Gentryville. Its claim to fame is that it's only about three miles from Abe Lincoln's boyhood home. My claim to fame is that my mother was born in a house that's now a historic Lincoln site house in that town. (It was a run-down tenant house at the time she was there.)

My stories are about my Place, my home on the Kentucky River. But Gentryville is a secondary place, one I closely identify with, and one that also feels like home.

All of Mom's family has been there since pioneer days. Over the years, I've gotten a lot of enjoyment wandering and exploring the back roads, the little communities, and the family cemeteries of Spencer and Warrick Counties, all in search of my own Hoosier roots.

My Granddaddy Crews grew up on a family farm originally obtained through public land sales in the 1830s. It appears to have been a rather hardscrabble existence. He followed the wheat harvest in the Great

Plains and told me stories of hopping freight trains in the 1920s. He and my grandmother got married on a neighbor's front porch shortly after the start of the Depression, and they barely survived off the income from tenant farming and trapping for the first decade of their married life. Things got better during the war, when he and his brother drove to Indianapolis during the week to work in a defense-related factory. After the war, he took a job as a house painter, which provided a reasonable income for the rest of his working career.

Granddaddy wasn't particularly interested in church. He'd take my granny there on Sunday morning, and then he and his brother and a couple friends would go play cards under a nearby railroad trestle until it was time to go pick her up. (I've wondered, why there, of all places! I have no idea, but Granddaddy's sister showed me the actual trestle location many years after he died.)

I visited them a lot as I was growing up, spending a couple weeks at a time with them, so I got to know my granddad well. I don't remember him particularly spending any time entertaining me, but I tagged along with him when I could.

Granddaddy was a racoon hunter—they called it "coon hunting"—and he had some pens behind the house where he kept his hunting dogs. One was a Bluetick Coonhound that would start barking in the middle of the night. Granddaddy would get up, open the door, and holler out, "Blue, dry up out there!" His hollering never did much good.

I went out hunting with him a few nights when I was there during the winter. He and a couple of his friends would go out nearly every night. There's a vast swampland in the area where he lived, and they knew it well and had the run of thousands of acres. They'd all wear a carbide head lamp, which emitted a very distinct, pungent, somewhat smoky odor. We'd walk out in the woods, and after a while they'd let the dogs loose and just sit down on a log and listen. Soon, one of the dogs would come across the trail of a racoon, and it would start barking (actually sounded like more of a baying) and follow the racoon's trail, barking the whole way. Granddaddy and his friends wouldn't get up in any hurry. They'd continue to sit and talk about which dog was the one on the trail.

Their conversations while sitting on the log were memorable. I recall a lot of quiet in the conversation. One would say something like, "Ol' Gray's picked up a scent." Then no one else would say anything for a while, and another one would mention another dog was on a trail, and then some more silence. They'd sit there, enjoying a cigarette and just seeming to enjoy each other's company.

It still amazes me that they could tell the dogs apart by their barks! Once one dog started, the others would follow it. After a while, their barks would sound different. Granddaddy and his friends knew they'd "treed" the raccoon, so they'd get up and go find the dogs. They'd finally get to the tree and shoot the animal, then start the process over again. They'd stay out till three or four in the morning, come home, get some sleep, and go out again the next night. They had a market for the hides, and they'd have a couple hundred pelts by the time the season ended.

I got my exploration gene from my granddaddy. He loved to drive around the back roads near his home. One of my fondest memories is riding with him in his 1963 cream-colored Ford Fairlane. With one arm hanging out the window, the other on the wheel with a cigarette between his fingers, and his ball cap cocked to one side, he'd whistle "Wolverton Mountain," a popular country song from about 1960. He'd whistle it at a slightly different beat than the song on the radio. He passed away in 1977, but I can still hear that song in the same beat he used.

He read westerns, and I still have his old hardbound Zane Gray westerns. As a boy, I wanted to be like my grandad, so I started reading those books, and even now, I love them.

When I was a kid, I looked up to my granddad, and nearly fifty years after his death, I still do. Thinking about it, I'm not sure why. He wasn't particularly ambitious. I'd be hard-pressed to point out any noticeably admirable characteristics. He was somewhat self-absorbed.

I think what I admire was his satisfaction with life. He got a great deal of enjoyment from his hunting. He'd lay back on the couch and spend a couple hours reading his western, or he'd sit back and intently listen to a baseball game on the radio. I remember how much he seemed to relish just sitting back and listening to his hounds bark, off in the distance, on a cold, frosty night. And I don't think I ever saw anyone savor a cigarette as he did.

He didn't have much, but he made do with what he had, and he was happy with it. I don't recall him ever complaining. And I have a great deal of respect for that.

⬦

Wendell Berry, a poet, novelist, essayist, farmer, and a friend, lives a few miles downstream from my Place. Since 1979, he has written poetry about early Sunday morning walks in the hillside woods overlooking his home and farm. *This Day: Collected Sabbath Poems* starts with:

> "I go among the trees and sit still.
> All my stirring becomes quiet
> around me like circles on water.
> My tasks lie in their places
> where I left them, asleep like cattle."

It's a beautiful description of what has given him peace and contentment over the years, and it serves as an example and an inspiration for me.

When I was remodeling my house, I spent a lot of time wiring the house for sound, running speaker wires into nearly every room. I mentioned earlier that my dad got annoyed with how much time I was spending doing something that he considered frivolous and unnecessary, and my wife tended to agree with him.

But I probably got more enjoyment from the extensive speaker system than anything else I did. I thoroughly enjoyed my music throughout the house and yard the fifteen or so years we lived there. It's one of the things I miss most about the house.

I don't think I had completely connected the dots at the time, but I was working hard on something I knew would provide some enjoyment and contentment for me. I love music. One of my favorite things was to sit out on the porch or by the fire pit at the Place and crank up the stereo on the outside speakers. Depending on my mood at the time, I might listen to Sinatra, Jimmy Buffett, Billie Holiday, Johnny Cash, or maybe some jazz or classical music, but it was almost always on. Sometimes just background, but oftentimes, truly listening and appreciating the singer's voice or the instrumentation.

Over time, I finally realized that this was something that Granddaddy Crews taught me. It has been a blessing to me, and I am thankful for the insight he unknowingly provided for me.

The Principle in Practice

One of the hardest things for a busy person to do is to make the time to proactively seek peace and fulfillment, to spend quality time with themselves. Putting out fires, fixing problems, keeping things moving–it's easy to get so caught up building our life and our business that we tend to forget to actually live the life we want that business to provide.

Matthew Kelly, in his book, *Slowing Down to the Speed of Joy*, states that "The speed and busyness of our lives stand in direct opposition to what we say matters most." We seldom pause to ask that deeper question: "Am I spending any meaningful time on the things that actually give me peace?"

Contentment is not accidental. It doesn't show up when you check everything off your to-do list for the day. You've got to build that into your day with choices that say, "This matters."

The first step is to simply name what brings you peace, what restores you. It might be a long walk, a hard workout, some spiritual reading in a favorite chair, or even a quiet cup of coffee before the rest of the house wakes up. Once you know what restores you, treat it like it matters, because it does. Put it on your calendar, just like every other commitment. Don't ever leave your peace to chance or squeeze it into the leftover margins of your day.

There is power in simple rituals that can keep you grounded. That cup of coffee. A deep breath or a simple prayer before a meeting. A five-minute walk. These sanity rituals can become an anchor on those days when everything's going haywire.

Another small shift is to develop a "Do-Not-Do" list, in order to protect yourself from what you will no longer tolerate. Peace and contentment sometimes come from subtraction. What do you need to *stop* doing? Maybe it's checking your emails after 8:00 p.m., or checking your social media before 8:00 a.m. Maybe it's working through lunch. Maybe it's no longer ignoring the quitting time reminder on your phone. Maybe it's not saying "yes" out of guilt or because of someone else's urgency. Whatever it is, setting boundaries is not selfish. Rather, it's protecting your time and energy and sanity, and your ability to show up well for the things that do matter.

Lastly, carve out one thing in your week that doesn't have anything to do with goals, or productivity, or growing your business, but rather something you do simply because it fills your soul. Give your full attention to it and just be there for it. It might be setting time to sit out and watch the sunset, or listen fully and completely to some music that you enjoy, or handwriting a note to someone you love. This can help to remind you why you are doing any of this in the first place.

Peace and contentment are the result of small decisions you make over time. Start making space for what matters to you.

How Others Have Put This to Work

A part-time landscaper was seriously considering quitting his job and focusing on building this new landscaping business he had started. It was a tempting idea for him—working outdoors, being his own boss, building something of his own, but before making the leap, he enrolled in a week-long, boot-camp-style business training I was holding.

The rigorous experience helped him do the hard mental work of weighing his options instead of just imagining the possibilities, and he came to a surprising conclusion. He realized walking away from his steady job was not the right move for him. While the idea of business ownership had its appeal, so did the life he already had. He understood that staying where he wasn't a sign of failure or avoiding a hard choice. It was a decision he made with intention, wisdom, and, ultimately, peace.

This decision has served him well, and he considers it successful. He still reflects on that week as a turning point, because it helped him see the value of the life he had already built.

A Question Worth Asking Yourself

What gives you peace? How long has it been since you spent meaningful time doing that?

_____

_____

_____

_____

_____

_____

The Pace of Contentment™

Running a business can take over your life, if you let it. I created *The Pace of Contentment™* to give you a starting point for noticing what brings you peace, what's getting in the way, and what small changes you can make now that could start making a difference. Help yourself actively slow down so you can enjoy the life you've been given with this tool at www.RootsandRiversBook.com/FreeTools.

How Others Have Put This to Work

A Virginia Fractional COO named Lisa had a business that was bringing in steady revenues and felt strong on the surface, but in her words, "It felt unpredictable." Most of her hours were spent on client work instead of building her business, and she was constantly second-guessing her own decisions. Without a clear way to explain what made her company different, she sometimes accepted clients who weren't aligned with her values, which created stress for both her and her team.

Lisa had a loosely defined set of values by which she operated her business. Through our work together, she was able to "sharpen and really drill down into" those values. Our conversations around better understanding her numbers and clearly articulating what made her value proposition unique helped her tie her decision-making back to the company she wanted to build, the values she held dear, and the competence and credibility she wanted to project.

Lisa states, "Excellence, to me, is doing right by our clients, while building our team at the same time, and just providing the most value we can within that context."

A turning point came when she chose to fire a client who made up a good portion of her monthly cash flow but didn't align with her values. That decision, though difficult, freed her to focus on the right clients and the right work. Because of the efforts we made in building her sales pipeline, she had a sense of peace with that decision. "I know I'm doing the right thing. I don't have that internal battle with myself."

She feels content with where she is now, believing herself to be growing in a way that allows her to build a strong long-term foundation for the business while simultaneously giving herself room to grow.

PRINCIPLE FIVE
Execute with Excellence

The Work It Takes to Keep
Everything Moving Smoothly

As a Kentucky farm boy, I've got an intimate connection with the seasonal rhythm of a burley tobacco farm. Although I haven't raised a tobacco crop in forty years, that rhythm is still in my blood. I particularly enjoy the July 4 holiday, because that was the holiday we celebrated growing up, with ice tea and the river, and no work. On Memorial Day, we were setting tobacco over that long weekend. The long Labor Day weekend was used to harvest tobacco. On Thanksgiving, and sometimes even on Christmas Day, depending on the weather, we'd have to work part of the day. On July 4, we played. That's my holiday!

An author I mentioned in the last chapter, Wendell Berry, has a whole series of novels that depict life in a rural tobacco community, and how the rhythms of the crop affect the whole rhythm of life in that community. (In fact, one of the greatest compliments I've ever received came from someone who said something I wrote reminded them of Mr. Berry.) Wendell's job as a writer is to reflect on those rhythms. Most people involved in tobacco production don't have much time to do that. I generally don't either, but because of Wendell, over the years, I've made time to occasionally ruminate over how the culture of the crop affects the whole lifestyle of the community.

I find something almost magical about it—how the land, the workers, the tools, the weather all come together to create that local rhythm. Because of Wendell, I've had the foresight to watch the process unfold in real time. It's simple to describe but difficult to do well. Transplants need to be put in the ground when the soil is in just the right condition, with the equipment working to deliver water to each transplant to keep it alive until it gets established on its own. Come harvest time, you need workers with the skill, as well as the speed and precision, to cut the individual plants and spear them on a stick to allow them to cure just right. Those sticks need to stay in the field for just the right amount of time to lose some weight from water evaporating, but not so long that the plants either get sunburned or start to rot from laying on the ground. Once these sticks are in the barn, the farmer needs to manage the doors of the barn to ventilate the barn and to let the right amount of humidity in the barn so the crop will cure slowly, but not so slowly that it starts to rot (houseburn in tobacco country vernacular). That requires a link between the weather and the farmer's skill in reading the conditions.

If any of these steps are rushed—if the weather doesn't cooperate, if the farmer is late doing the work because the equipment broke down, if the help doesn't show up—then the quality of the crop suffers. A small mistake can affect the entire harvest and the farmer's yearly revenues. The rhythm matters.

Central Kentucky has been the heart of burley tobacco production for generations. Farmers there have developed skills that are hard to match. They know the soil, the climate, and the exact timing for planting and harvesting in a way that produces leaves that are most desired by buyers. The farmers understand the curing process and how temperature and airflow in the barns affect the cure. These aren't skills someone can pick up quickly. They're unique to the region, valuable in the marketplace, and difficult for farmers in other regions to replicate. Farmers who master them can command better prices.

Core competencies operate on the same principle in business. These are the strengths in your company's skills, knowledge, or resources that are unique, valuable, and hard to copy. They are what give you an advantage in the market. Just like the farmers in Central Kentucky, identifying and developing these strengths allows you to focus your energy on what truly sets your business apart and produces results others cannot easily match.

Excellence shows up in the details. In my early days as a farm advisor, I visited a farmer I greatly admired, Harold Malcomb. The process for wintertime prep for the market involved taking each individual leaf off the tobacco stalk and putting a handful of these stripped leaves (called a hand) on a stick, with about a dozen of these hands on the stick presented to buyers. A completed stick needed to be squeezed together (pressed) to make efficient use of space. Harold would take as much as ten minutes for each of these sticks, turning leaves just so, in order to make the best presentation to the buyers as possible, and he taught his son Steve to do the same. It paid off, as Harold had one of the best-looking crops on the market, and he typically received the highest prices for his excellence.

The same applies to a business. Excellence is a clear standard of performance, applied consistently to every task. It's the measure of quality in every action your business takes.

Farmers measure their harvest. They track yields, they compare quality to previous seasons, and they notice patterns that affect the next planting. These metrics guide their decisions about equipment repair vs. replacement, about labor needs, and about varieties to plant. Businesses need the same approach. Metrics show whether systems work, whether people are applying their strengths, and whether standards are being met. They allow you to correct mistakes before they affect outcomes.

We'll discuss all this in the next few chapters. When it comes together, the work of your business resembles a well-run farm. Strengths are applied in the right places. Standards define how work is done. Metrics show what is working and what needs adjustment. Every action adds to the results, and the effort produces measurable progress. Miss one piece, and the results suffer. Get them all in place, and the work flows with rhythm, precision, and efficiency.

CHAPTER 16

Best Place for a Campground

I've already told you about how my grandfather Strohmeier came to hear of this great fishing camp on the Kentucky River, a few miles north of Frankfort. It was right at the mouth of the Elkhorn Creek, so they could try their luck on two very different streams. Pop Strohmeier said that sounded like a good idea, so they started planning their trip.

Today, that trip between our homeplace and his plumbing store on Bardstown Road in Louisville takes about an hour, but in the 1920s, it was a major journey, and they would have taken Pop's Model T truck. The road from Louisville (the biggest city in the state) to Frankfort was a decent highway, but the twelve or so miles from Frankfort to the fishing camp was mostly a gravel road that followed the original horse path. We still have pictures of his branded truck sitting outside his store, and I can imagine that truck traveling these narrow, winding roads in rural Franklin County. The trip would have taken close to three hours at the time.

When they finally arrived at this remote location, they would have found an angler's paradise. The owners, the Quires, had big dreams. They had built this fishing camp to attract a lot of visitors. They recognized it was a sportsman's dream; with a setting at the confluence of two waters with widely different temperaments, a fisherman could relax on the flatwater of a major river, or—on the same day—try their skills in the riffles of a lively creek.

When they first drove in, they would have found a big three-story hotel on the property, as well as several rustic cabins overlooking the river. Next to the hotel, they would have been surprised to find a silo. The location had been the shipping port for farmers in the area to load their livestock on a packet boat to ship downstream to markets in Louisville, so there was already a launch ramp into the river; all they had to do was rent a boat, and they were set for several days' worth of fishing.

Pop fell in love with the place, and when the opportunity came to purchase it a decade later, he jumped at the chance. While he had a successful plumbing business, he recognized the unique opportunity this place presented. As my dad grew up, he also recognized the possibilities this place offered. Not only was there access to the two streams, but there was plenty of space for development. Pop bought a fishing camp in the 1930s, but fifty years later, this type of retreat had evolved into campgrounds. Dad visited some over the years, and he noticed how tightly packed most campgrounds were. He saw the opportunity to provide something most other campgrounds did not have: elbow room.

In the early 1980s, he started developing his own dream: a scenic campground in which families could come and have space to run and romp. They could rent a boat, or a canoe, and enjoy either the tranquility of the smooth serene river or the energy of a fast moving creek. It was a perfect adult playground.

And it remains so to this day. He had campers that rented sites in those first years that stayed for decades. He ran the campground for forty years, finally selling it in his nineties when he was unable to take care of it anymore. Some of those original campers were still there during that transition.

$$\diamondsuit$$

The year I ran the campground, I don't know how many people commented about the beauty of the place, the space their kids had to room to run wild and soak up the outdoors, and how much fun it was to enjoy the streams. We had what I call a core competency: a strength that was uniquely ours and couldn't be duplicated by someone else. No other campground in the state (of which we were aware) had marina access to two different streams. A number of them are on a lake or a river or a creek, but no one else had the unique capabilities of enjoying two different bodies of water. Few campgrounds had as much space available as we did to allow for huge campsites, as well as open space around the campsites and wooded areas on the property with trails for them to hike.

This allowed us to provide a lot of services for our customers. When they camped with us, they received value they couldn't get anywhere else. They could launch a boat or a pontoon, and go fishing or water skiing or tubing. We could provide moonlight canoe trips. We could put in canoes upstream, and they could take their time coming downstream and take out at our place, without having to wait for someone to come pick them up. We could sell tubes, and they could tube down the creek; with the horseshoe bend location, they could take out at our launch site, and if they wanted to, they could walk back to the put-in point and do it again.

The location was great for a campground, and it made for a unique competitive advantage.

The Principle in Practice

Rob Ryan, in his book *Smartups*, states that most entrepreneurs "get so wrapped up in their product that it's hard for them to think in terms of what they do best." But anyone who wants to build a successful business has to do so.

A core competency is something you do better than anyone else—those areas of your business where you add the most value. It's what makes people choose you. Think of it as your unique edge.

It could be a skill, a process, a relationship, or even something in your culture, like how committed your team is. It's not tied to a specific product, but it does shape the kinds of products or services you're able to offer. For example, Honda's strength isn't just cars or lawnmowers; it's their small-engine technology. Sony's strength is miniaturized electronics. These are the building blocks behind everything else they do.

You may have several competitive advantages, but most businesses only have one or two true core competencies. As a small business owner, it's important to figure out what you do really well, what sets you apart and can't easily be copied.

To identify that, ask yourself a few things: What do I do better than anyone else? What do my customers say about me, and why do they keep coming back? Then, look behind those answers and determine what strengths or skills are making those things possible.

A true core competency will support a variety of things you could sell and open the door to more than one market.

When you've named your core competency, new product or service ideas will start to take shape. It becomes a foundation for future growth.

If you can't clearly name one yet, that's okay. Start by looking at where you have an edge—any small advantage you can build on. With time and focus, that can grow into a true core strength.

A Question Worth Asking Yourself

What is it that you do better than anyone else? What makes you YOU?

_____

_____

_____

_____

_____

_____

_____

Core Competency Compass™

Sometimes it's hard to see what sets you apart when you're busy trying to keep everything going. I've put together a simple worksheet to help you think through what you do best, what your customers value most, and how that might shape the future of your business. Visit www.RootsandRiversBook.com/FreeTools to download the _Core Competency Compass™_ to start sorting out what makes you unique.

CHAPTER 17

Mom's Quilts

I suspect we all have a tendency to take our parents' unique skills for granted. I know I did. It took years before I realized how talented of an artist my mom was.

She was a quilter. Late in her life, my brother Kevin and I set up a display of her quilts at a local gallery. It was a job hanging them all, and we worked at it without really seeing the big picture of what we were doing—until we got done. When I took a step back to see the finished display, it caught my breath. WOW! This was amazing! All those quilts hanging on the wall helped me understand what an incredible body of art Mom had created over a lifetime.

If I had to pick one family heirloom only and dispose of all else, I would keep the collection of quilts she and my grandmother crafted.

Granny learned how to quilt from her mother; it was a skill nearly every girl from a poor rural community in the early 1900s learned.

Granny's mother did it because she had to, but Granny loved it, and she taught my mom to love it.

In the early 1990s, Mom set up a quilt show to display all Granny's quilts at her hometown of Gentryville, Indiana; there were about forty quilts on display. My dad built display racks, and once all the quilts were hung, I videotaped my mom asking Granny about the story behind each quilt. The stories were great; I learned the details of Granny's everyday life and struggles as she recounted her memories, but what touched me most was quietly watching her walk around by herself while everyone else was busy setting up for a reception. She was admiring her own work displayed in one place, but I sensed a feeling of awe and humility in this tiny, elderly lady, who had never before been publicly recognized, that someone would go to the effort of honoring her this way.

In the fall of 2016, I returned the favor for my mom, displaying about fifty quilts she had made over the course of her lifetime at a gallery hosted by a church in downtown Frankfort.

While I've always appreciated the quilts, that exhibition made me realize what a treasure they were. Mom's quilts were all of a traditional style, and all hand-quilted. She took great pride in her mother's abilities and always tried to emulate them, noting with admiration that Granny could make twelve stitches an inch, which was something of a badge of honor for quilters.

Shortly before Mom's dementia from Parkinson's started, I inventoried all her quilts, including all the photos and stories behind each quilt. I found out Mom and Granny worked together on many of these quilts over the years. In one case, shortly after my grandfather died,

Mom had pieced a quilt and was planning on finishing it herself, but she decided to ask Granny to quilt it, as a way to keep her busy and her mind occupied as a way to deal with her grief. It's a beautiful quilt, with a lot of white area that shows some intricate detail, maybe Granny's masterpiece. A few years later, Granny saw the quilt at Mom's house and asked about it. She didn't remember quilting it. It had served the purpose of keeping Granny's hands busy, but she had no recollection of the actual quilt she'd worked on.

Mom's masterpiece was a memorial quilt she made for Kevin's teenage son Ben. It was her way of dealing with her grief from his accidental death. Each block was a different flower she had designed herself. Ben was a lover of nature and the outdoors, and she felt this was the best way she could honor him and his legacy.

Mom often used her quilting as an emotional outlet. One fall, she'd gotten a set of wind chimes and had Dad hang them up outside behind her sewing room. That winter was particularly cold and windy, and she continually heard those chimes in her sewing room while she was working. They were soothing to her. She had collected some patterns over time that had a wind theme, so she put several of these together into her own design and named the quilt "Wind Song."

After Dad passed away, Francie and I, and Kevin and his wife Luna, were going through his house, beginning to clean up and start on the necessary disposal of belongings. Luna, who is a fabric artist herself, was going through Mom's sewing room cabinets. She called Kevin and me, saying she'd found something intriguing. She'd come across Mom's planning drawer. In looking through the patterns she'd saved, and templates of designs, it confirmed to us her incredible artistry. Luna found where she had cut out and put pieces of fabric together as a way of testing colors, like a painter might do on a palette. She had taken various designs she liked and experimented drawing them out in different ways on scraps of paper.

We also found notes that gave us a glimpse of her thoughts as she designed a quilt for a specific reason, or for a person she wanted to give it to. For instance, she had a photo of Uncle Eddie standing in the midst of some flowering shrubs with several pattern designs and some fabric samples that matched the colors in the photo.

Not only was she technically skilled as a quilter, but she also created her own designs, her own piece of art.

We gathered her collection of quilts, which included some of Granny's quilts, as well as a few quilts made by our great grandparents (one was signed by Granny's mother and dated, "Effie Pace 1936"). One evening, relaxing with some bourbon, the four of us sat down and admired each quilt, both the design and the craftsmanship, reviewing the story we knew behind each one, and decided which of us would take each quilt. Kevin and I both feel that, in a way, it's our responsibility to preserve their legacies.

In my office, I have several of her quilts displayed. "Wind Song" is hanging on a wall rack my dad built for her in our hallway. It's a daily reminder of her and the craftsmanship she displayed.

⬦

Mom's and Granny's quilts showed a high level of craftsmanship and a dedication to excellence in their work. I remember Mom ripping out stitches when she didn't meet her own standards.

I like to think I picked up that trait from them. I've done some woodworking and furniture refinishing over the years, and I'm really anal on doing it right. In my position as a farm advisor, I made presentations and wrote articles, and I made sure the details were nearly perfect. I once built a deck on our house, and a friend of mine jokingly commented that a tornado might blow away my house, but it wouldn't stand a chance against a deck I'd built!

I understand quality and excellence can sometimes go too far. Perfectionism can slow progress. I've occasionally missed some opportunities because I let the pursuit of perfection get in the way of something being good enough.

It's important enough to me that excellence is one of my own stated values in my business, seeking curiosity, creativity, craftsmanship, and innovation in ourselves and in all with whom we work.

Excellence takes on many forms in a business. For me, it's how my systems hold together, how I treat my team members and the results I expect from them, and how I handle problems and adapt to unexpected changes. It's setting strong standards and living out these standards daily.

A big part of excellence has involved the service I try to provide my customers, whether it was the quality of free programs I provided my farm clients, the service we provided to campground customers, or the coaching expertise I now provide for my business coaching clients. My intent is that this standard of excellence becomes the culture of my company.

The Principle in Practice

Excellence in business not only includes the goals you set, but maybe more importantly, how you get there. Its evidence is found in the details, in how your team works, how your systems run, and how your customers are treated. It shows up in the small invisible everyday actions of the business—steady habits, clear communication, people doing what they say they'll do.

Different people show excellence in different ways. A technician might do careful, accurate work. A manager might keep the team focused and steady. A staff member might spot problems before they grow. When something goes wrong, a strong business responds quickly and takes responsibility. That builds trust, both within and outside the business.

Customers notice the finished product, but they also remember how easy it was to work with you and how well you keep your word. When they feel respected, understood, and supported, they are far more likely to come back and become a regular customer.

Tom Peters states in *The Pursuit of Wow!*, "You will be remembered, in the long haul, for the quality of your work, not the quantity of your work. No one evaluates Picasso based on the number of paintings he churned out."

If you want to bring more excellence into your business, start by looking at what's already working. Where are things running smoothly? Where do you see strong habits or good communication? Then ask yourself, where is that missing? Pick one place to start and raise the standard.

Excellence is a choice. Over time, those choices will shape your business into one you can be proud of.

A Question Worth Asking Yourself

How do you define "Excellence" in your business?

_____

_____

_____

_____

_____

_____

Raising the Standard Self-Review™

If you'd like a little help thinking through how excellence shows up, or doesn't, in your business, here's a worksheet I've created to help you take stock of what's already working, what might need some attention, and where you might quietly raise the bar.

Visit www.RootsandRiversBook.com/FreeTools to download _Raising the Standard Self-Review™_. It's a helpful way to step back and make sure your daily standards continue to reflect the kind of business you're working to build.

CHAPTER 18

Flood Data

I talked about the very personal experiences I've had with flooding. It was important to know what the predictions were, so we knew what to prepare for.

The major floods in Frankfort, just upstream from us, were in 1937, 1978, and 1997 (and 2025), where flood levels were carefully measured, so the flood predictions were important guides for us.

After we moved to our homeplace, I found myself paying close attention to high water levels and predictions. Not only was I concerned with my own home, but I needed to be ready to help Dad move campers out.

I mentioned earlier that on average, the water didn't get into my house but about once every thirty years. Our danger level was about forty-four feet. But the campground was on much lower ground. The water would start getting into the campground at about thirty feet, so campers would need to get out before then. That happened about every five or so years.

Whenever we would start getting heavy rains, particularly in the spring, my dad and I would pay attention to the flood predictions. We noticed the waters would crest at our place about nine hours after it crested in Frankfort. I started taking pictures of water levels at particular landmarks on the Place, so we could better use that information for our own planning purposes. As we moved people out, we also noted how long that evacuation would take, so we could have a better idea of how long we'd have for future flooding.

One July 4th weekend, we had uncommonly heavy rain for mid-summer. Campers were out in full force, and as they watched the water rise in the bottom below the campground, they started to worry. Flood crest predictions were twenty-eight feet, two feet short of our danger zone. Campers kept calling the office, asking if they needed to start packing to leave. But by having this data and knowing these local landmarks, we were confident in making the call that no one needed to move. Sure enough, it crested about two feet before it reached the campground.

After that crest, the campers all breathed a sigh of relief, and that was the talk of the weekend. They all had their own flood stories to take home with them. Knowing some of these folks, I fully expect some of these stories became considerably embellished with each telling, over time.

$$\diamondsuit$$

When we talk about data and numbers, which is inherent in a discussion about measurements, I find that people mostly fall into two categories: those who are passionate about numbers and how they work, and those who are panic-stricken!

I tend to fall into the first category. I love to try to figure out what the numbers are telling me.

I've also learned these numbers can provide peace.

During the fifteen or so years I lived at my Place, we had two floods that got near the house—close enough that we had flood water in our unfinished concrete basement.

By having this data, studying it, and paying close attention to what it meant, we realized that, both times, we didn't need to worry about moving everything out of our house. The water was up over the road, so we were stranded except by boat. With that, we didn't have anyplace we could go. I helped dad move the campers out, and after that, we just sat in our side yard looking at the much-closer river and enjoyed life. Much to the chagrin of our adult kids, we got out in a canoe and paddled through the campground and the fields that were now covered with water, avoiding only the main current in the river, and just enjoyed being river rats! We took selfies of us in the canoe fifteen feet from our back door and laughed about our new "Strohmeier Beachfront Properties."

We had a sense of peace knowing we were personally safe from the flooding.

The Principle in Practice

That same kind of peace is possible in business. When you take time to understand the numbers, when you know what to look for and what it means, you're no longer at the mercy of surprise. You may still get some high water—the data doesn't change the situation—but you'll know how high the water's likely going to get. You'll know when action is truly necessary, and it becomes less worrisome.

There are all kinds of measurements you could use, but generally, you want to focus on just a few. These are what Verne Harnish, in his book *Mastering the Rockefeller Habits*, calls Critical Numbers, which "represents a key short-term focus in the company that will have the most impact on the future" of the company.

The key, and the challenge, is picking the most important numbers. They aren't just financial numbers; they reflect on how work gets done and where energy should go.

Your business has to make money, so start by looking at what drives your revenue, profit, and customer satisfaction. Think through what has to happen from the first customer interaction all the way to getting paid. Each step adds value, but depending on your strengths, some steps matter more than others. Focus on the ones that most impact your success. Ask yourself: What's the one thing in this series of steps that must stay healthy for the business to thrive?

Net profit is critical, but you can't control it directly. What you can control are the actions that drive it, like lead flow or conversion rates. Look for the activity or behavior that produces the bulk of your revenue, is repeatable, is within your control, and is trackable in real time. A quick test: If that number dropped, would the business be in trouble right away?

Once you've found that key driver, break it down by function: marketing, sales, operations, HR, and so on. Each one has a core purpose. Ask yourself: What activity in this area matters most? What number could tell me every week whether it's working? Look for leading indicators, those numbers that give you a heads-up on what's about to happen, not just what's already happened.

Get your team involved in figuring this out. Test each metric. Is it easy to track? Does it change behavior? If not, keep digging. Tie the numbers to a clear goal. Without a goal, tracking numbers is just busywork. With a goal, you have a tool for growth.

Once you have the right numbers, track them weekly or monthly, and share them with your team. Help everyone see how their role impacts the score. Make the numbers visible, like a scoreboard. Expect some trial and error. Drop metrics that don't give timely insight or that don't drive results. Focus on the few that really move the business forward.

How Others Have Put This to Work

The owner of a small manufacturing plant in my hometown was struggling; Anthony was doing a good bit of the grunt work in the plant, which did not allow him time to do the management work of growing the business. As he said, he was "everywhere but nowhere at the same time," working on whatever seemed important at the moment. In addition, he didn't have a clear sense of where his money was going. All he knew was, the business was losing money.

This stress followed him home, affecting his time with his family, because he didn't have the energy for anything outside the business.

We started working together, and our first priority was getting spending under control. He did that by creating a written chart of accounts, making sure the business didn't pay for personal expenses, starting to use a cash flow budget, and renegotiating with suppliers for better terms. He also completed a time audit, which showed where his hours were going, which, in turn, allowed him to free up time for higher value work.

All it took was studying some numbers that were important to his business. And the resulting actions he took from that study turned out to be wildly successful. Within three months, his bank balance had increased fivefold, and he went from a net loss to a very reasonable and comfortable net profit within a year.

He's also gained back control of his life. He's no longer doing the heavy lifting at work, but rather delegating jobs he used to do to employees and allowing them the benefit of figuring out the details.

He's been able to spend more time with his family. He's less stressed, and his health has improved. And his perspective has shifted, in that it's changed the way he thinks about money and business—in fact, the entire way he thinks about what's most important in his life.

A Question Worth Asking Yourself

What are the three most important leading critical numbers you should be tracking to know if your business is on track for the growth you want?

_____

_____

_____

_____

_____

Freedom Metrics Planner™

It can be hard to figure out which numbers actually matter and which ones just make you feel busy. The *Freedom Metrics Planner*™ can help you think through the key parts of your business, narrow in on what really drives results, and choose a few numbers you can actually use to make better decisions. Visit www.RootsandRiversBook.com/FreeTools to download this worksheet so you can cut through the noise and start tracking what actually moves your business forward.

Emotional Flood Trauma Postscript

Ironically, in the process of writing this book, in April 2025, my hometown was inundated with one of the worst floods it has ever experienced. The homeplace we moved from three years ago had water in it up to the fourth step going upstairs. My dad had to move out of his house, the house I grew up in, which had water in it for the first time ever.

When we moved to Virginia, one of the factors in favor of the move was that we would no longer have to worry about a flood. But that weekend, I found that is not the case. It hurt. I had a deep sorrow for what happened to my old house. I was truly saddened for the new owner, who had made it a vacation rental home. When we lived there, I felt so strongly about our Place that I wanted to share it with others. This new use, as a destination for travelers, allowed my dream to be carried on through someone else. And now, my treasured home, my meticulous renovation efforts, my well-tended landscape, my tranquil view of the river, and my peaceful retreat from the commotion of the world around me was covered with water, mud, sludge, and trash.

On a more practical level, I was concerned about my dad's physical and emotional state. As I prepared to leave for Kentucky to start cleaning up Dad's house, I was also a bit worried about my own abilities to rip out carpets and hose down walls; I was thirty years older than when I did this before!

After a day's worth of cleanup with Kevin, we called it quits for the day because we were too tired to do anything else. We headed into town to our favorite watering hole, where we sat and traded war stories (or shall I say, flood stories) with other people who were also worn out from their own cleaning up.

I realized something that week that I think I already inherently knew. We were, in a sense, a little community of people with shared interests who could get together after working through some bad experiences, and laugh about it and commiserate together. We all had been through this before, and we accepted it and looked at it as a major annoyance we had to get through.

I also ran into some people that had not dealt with a flood before, including the couple that bought our house. They drove in while we were cleaning Dad's house, so they could see the damage. I immediately noticed that they seemed to be almost shell-shocked at the amount of water and at the immensity of the job of cleaning up.

When we sold the house, I had left the written flood plan with the new owner. Over the past three years, he called me occasionally to ask some questions about where something was or how we did things. I helped him talk through concerns about other river crests that weren't so high. He mostly followed the plan, but he just wasn't prepared for the initial devastation that he saw with three feet of water in the house.

I sensed this from other people I ran into that week, for whom this was also their first flood. There may be no greater mess than what several feet of muddy flood water can cause. The demoralizing experience of someone seeing, for the first time, their ruined home—the soggy carpet, the sagging drywall, the mud-laden water-soaked furniture, the family heirlooms that have been destroyed—can leave someone sick to their stomach. They're devastated by their loss, they're overwhelmed with the idea of this massive cleanup effort, and they don't have a clue as to where to start.

$$\Leftrightarrow$$

At times, I've had conversations with business owners in which I've gotten a sense of that same shell-shocked feeling, in that they've gotten to the point where they feel in over their heads and see no way out. They feel defeated. They know something's got to change, but they don't know how to make those changes. They're reeling and don't know where to turn.

When this happens, when the pressure of challenges reaches a breaking point, it's hard to see a way forward. But there is no challenge that's completely new—there's always been someone who's been there before, who's already dealt with that challenge and learned from it. They've already figured it out and found a way through. The key is knowing when and where to lean on that experience, to learn from someone else's perspective.

The experience with the flood reminded me of the value of working with someone who has dealt with it firsthand. The person that bought our house couldn't believe the amount of damage he was seeing, but thanks to my insight, drawn from the perspective of having lived through it, he moved quickly to start cleaning up.

Whether it's rebuilding after a flood or navigating tough moments in business, finding someone who has already walked that road can make all the difference. You don't have to face it alone. There's always someone who can walk beside you, helping you to get over these hurdles, making what once seemed insurmountable suddenly achievable.

The Principle in Practice

There is a wealth of people out there who can help you grow your business, people who have done it themselves and are happy to share their own knowledge and insights.

You may be fortunate enough to know someone personally who has had a similar business and is willing to pass on some of their own personal experience and insights to you. But moving past a personal friend, you've got several broad options for gaining help.

Free services, like the Small Business Development Centers in most states, provide help in business planning, generally focused on the financial side of the business.

Business consultants provide expert advice for specific projects, based on that consultant's own particular industry experience. It's up to you to decide on whether or not to take that advice and how to implement it.

Business mentors can be helpful, particularly to start-ups. These relationships are typically informal and rooted in personal experience, with limited structure or accountability.

Business coaches, on the other hand, are more goal-driven and more structured than a mentoring relationship. You and the coach agree on some clear goals, and the coach holds you accountable while offering how-to resources and encouragement to help you move forward.

A good coach is not going to tell you what to do. They help you see past the immediate obstacles, so that you can envision the possibilities for your business. A good coach helps you grow the way you want to grow. When you're stuck, a good coach may offer some ideas, but the direction always stays in your hands.

How Others Have Put This to Work

A talented solopreneur coach named Patti had built a business around a skill in which she excelled and had a national reputation for her abilities. Despite all her efforts, crazy hours, and constant travel, the business wasn't growing the way she'd hoped. She was exhausted, barely breaking even, and unsure how to move forward. Deep down, she feared if she took a close look, she might have to admit the business wouldn't make it.

I helped her take that close look and figure out ways to make it succeed. By working through a clear structure, she started making decisions more intentionally.

One of the first big shifts came when she began tracking key performance indicators that actually mattered to her. She'd never really known her numbers before, but once she did, it changed the way she saw her business. It gave her more control, and it gave her hope.

What had once felt overwhelming began to feel doable, and she started gaining confidence and a renewed sense of purpose. She stated that it forced her to be honest with herself, and while that was hard, the clarity of what she gained far outweighed the uncomfortable part of the process.

She told me, "Coaching has improved my life. It reinforced to me that my business has tremendous value to bring to the world, and it has helped me become excited again about the potentials it offers."

A Question Worth Asking Yourself

What are the most important issues that are holding you back from reaching your business objectives?

_____

_____

_____

_____

Your Own Riverbank Strategy Session™

Through this book, I've described numerous business lessons I've learned through life at my Place, from my Kentucky riverbank. I've suggested what you, as the reader, might be able to glean from my own experiences, and I trust that you have gained some valuable insights from my own stories and lessons learned. With each one of these stories and lessons, I've provided a simple tool you can use that can serve as a guide for you to apply these lessons to your own business and your own life. If you haven't done so yet, you can download all these tools here, at www.RootsAndRiversBook.com/FreeTools.

I hope they have inspired you to make whatever needed changes you need to make.

There's a lot of ideas here. Many of them will require some thought. Many of them will require a healthy dose of imagination. And I know that sometimes, particularly when things are not going as well as you'd like, imagination can be a problem.

And when that imagination is a problem, it becomes hard just knowing how to start. And because of that—I know from my own personal experience—day-to-day work gets in the way, and inertia will quickly take over, and you won't get started. And you'll miss out on being able to do those things, those personal and business-building things, that you can't do because you have not made those changes.

So let me help you with that. Let me help you get started. I'll be happy to provide you with a complimentary one-hour *Your Own Riverbank Strategy Session*™ to help you work through the most pressing challenge that's holding you back. Think of it as a quiet moment on a virtual riverbank to step back, sort things out, and figure out a better way forward. No sales pitch and no further obligation on your part; this is just one way that I can show you my appreciation for paying attention to my stories.

Maybe I can help you reflect on how your own story has helped you grow. Maybe we can discuss how you can apply this PLACE framework within your own business. And maybe we can just talk about how one of these stories of my Place particularly resonates with you.

If you'd like to take me up on this, schedule your Riverbank Strategy Call here, or go to www.25withKim.com and schedule it from there. I'm looking forward to hearing from you.

Note to the Reader:

I've noticed over time that the business books that most resonate with me are ones that tell a story to get a point across. Patrick Lencioni does a beautiful job of conveying his ideas with a fable in all of his books. I use Michael Gerber's *The E Myth Revisited* as a starting point for all my coaching clients, because of the great way he outlines the need for business systems with a continual story. Setting up a Lean Program, a Japanese-inspired efficiency system, makes for some incredibly boring reading, but Eliyahu Goldratt's novel *The Goal,* about putting this in place, is a riveting tale. I learned far more about Lean Systems through this enjoyable read than I ever did by reading some respected textbooks on the concept. Bob Burg and John David Mann's *The Go-Giver* shifted my entire mindset about my values and how I did business. And it did so by telling a story. These have all helped reaffirm to me the idea that storytelling is a perfect way to teach a lesson. And I hope that I have done this well for you, as a reader.

I've hoped to paint a picture for you in some words. But for those very visual people who need to see the picture itself, here's a few photos of my Place:

Our Old Kentucky Home, painting by cousin Steve Tincher, 2023

Lonnie Quire's Mayflower hotel and Fishing Camp, ca.1927

Strohmeier family at homeplace, ca. 1949

Fishing camp river overlook, ca. 1955

Hompelace, author and brother Kevin on front porch, ca. 1964

Uncle Eddie,
Guadalcanal, ca. 1944

Uncle Eddie at
homeplace, ca. 1994

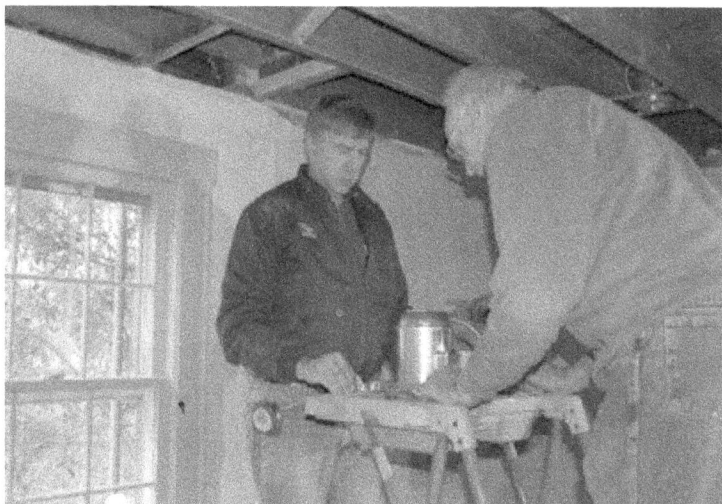

Kim and Dave Strohmeier remodeling the homeplace, 2006

Flooded homeplace, 2025

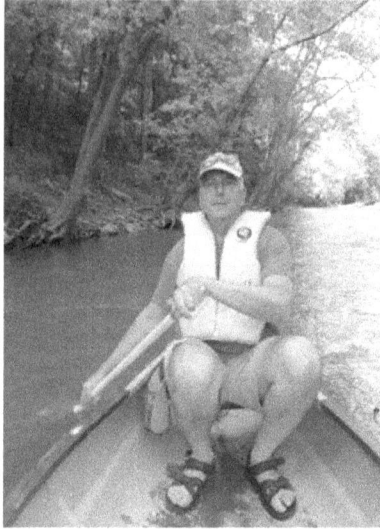

Author paddling on the Elkhorn Creek, ca. 2015

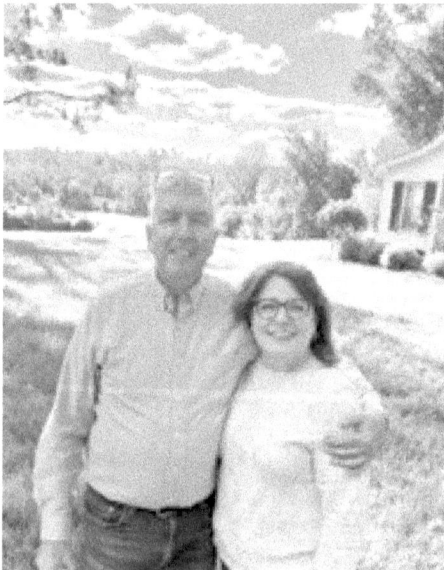

Author and wife Francie in front yard of homeplace, 2021